FROM WOUND TO WISDOM

A SHAMANIC APPROACH TO HEALING EMOTIONAL TRAUMA

ALBERTO CURCIO LINARES

DEDICATION

This book is dedicated to all the brave men and women who have the courage to listen and follow the guidance and wisdom of their hearts.

CONTENTS

HOW TO USE THIS BOOK

This is a reference book and a healing tool. The information presented here took me many years to develop. The viewpoints, concepts, and exercises will prompt you to examine reality from various perspectives. You will find I revisit some points from different angles throughout the book. The reason for my repetition is twofold. First, reinforcement of these concepts helps ensure they penetrate deep into your consciousness. Second, when you refer back to certain sections, I return to concepts that have been previously discussed to illustrate how they connect to the topic at hand.

Before diving into the spiritual healing practices I describe, I recommend first reading the whole book to familiarize yourself with the full scope of inner work I am presenting. Then revisit each chapter to help you integrate its concepts and lessons into your daily life – understanding them mentally, feeling them emotionally, and applying them physically. Take your time as you read Chapter I; develop a full understanding of the Universal Principles, and how to apply them, before moving on to the second chapter, which offers strategies for identifying and resolving past wounds, trauma, or conditioning. The third chapter will help you develop specific practices to support your healing. If you find yourself feeling unclear, or stuck on a certain concept, take some time and revisit it later. All this information can be a lot to digest at once. As you allow the concepts to percolate in your awareness, you will be able to make the necessary connections, enabling you to fully understand the perspectives I am sharing.

Disclaimer, in Chapter IV I introduce some traditional Indigenous spiritual practices, including the use of plant medicine, like Ayahuasca. If this section doesn't resonate with you, feel free to skip it. The point of this section is to illustrate the diversity of practices humans have historically used to connect with our spirituality.

Of course, there are positive and negative implications to such traditions becoming more mainstream and trendy. For instance, as the use of Ayahuasca has become more widespread globally, many people have been able to experience its healing power and connect with the sacredness of Mother Earth's gifts. This has helped many to care more about our natural environment, which is increasingly at risk of human-caused destruction. On the flip side, the increasing interest in Ayahuasca has tempted opportunistic people to take advantage of the trend for profit. Some who facilitate Ayahuasca "healing circles" are not prepared to do so, and cause more harm than healing. Those who do receive the proper traditional training necessary to facilitate Ayahuasca ceremonies have a responsibility to give back and support their teachers, honoring the sacredness of the tradition these practitioners carry and reciprocating the sharing of its healing potential. This ensures a continued relationship with the tradition and the ancestral lands where the sacred plants originated. Anyone who chooses to participate in traditional plant medicine ceremonies should carefully research the facilitator's experience, training, ethics, and connection to the Amazon jungle. Equipped with this information, potential participants will be assured of supporting facilitators with shared values, who will ensure their well-being during ceremonies.

PREFACE

I don't recall exactly what age I was when I realized that something was inherently wrong with the way I was living. Growing up in Venezuela's bustling capital, Caracas, I naturally believed that all life had to offer was found in a city. Anything "under-developed," including nature, seemingly lacked the necessary conditions to prosper.

My Catholic school upbringing further confused me. Throughout elementary and high school, I was ridden with the guilt ingrained in me by the Church's philosophies and teachings. At 15, I began to question what I was being taught. Increasingly, I felt that there was a different way of living, a different way of being. While I still believed I would go to hell if I didn't pray, just as the priests had taught me, the rebel within me was awakening. I stopped believing those priests when I graduated from high school. After a couple of years of friction with my parents, I realized that venturing out on my own was the only way to re-imagine life under my own direction.

I left Venezuela and moved to the Canary Islands when I was 21. I needed a whole ocean between my home country and myself. In this newfound space, I surfed, explored nature, and began learning about eastern philosophies. I read about Hinduism and Buddhism, which I found dense and over-whelming. At a friend's suggestion, I read about Taoism and Zen, and then I began to understand what I was looking for. In both philosophies, nature is the teacher and the place to seek guidance. This concept resonated with me deeply and was further imprinted upon me by Carlos Castaneda's book *The Teachings of Don Juan*, which introduced me to the incredible world of shamanism. It would be seven years before I would experience shamanic practices for myself, but the seedling idea had been planted: someday I would immerse myself more fully in that world.

Learning about shamanism also re-ignited an interest in, and admiration for, the Indigenous people who practiced it. In Venezuela there are more than twenty Indigenous groups, many of which continue to live traditionally and sustainably in different areas of the country.

I yearned to live more in balance with nature, as they did, so I sought inspiration and knowledge about how to do so. Throughout my travels in Central America, I experimented with psilocybin mushrooms, consuming them intuitively in natural settings. With each use, I became increasingly connected with nature, so much that I began seeing her as the only teacher and true wisdom keeper. I knew I was just begin-ning to scratch the surface of the shamanic world.

Even with the realization that nature was my greatest teacher, I still continued to pursue a path I thought might lead to success, however I grew increasingly unhappy, frustrated, and angry at myself and the world. I went to university in California and found myself in a marriage that left a bitter taste in my mouth. In hindsight, I realize I was unhappy because I was continuing a childhood pattern: letting others' opinions control me, instead of trusting my own intuition.

Around this time, a dear friend told me about his experience participating in a sacred ceremony in Venezuela during which he consumed Yagé, also known as Ayahuasca. As he shared his experience, I knew right away that this was what I was yearning for: a reconnection with nature and a deeper knowledge of healing shamanic rituals. A year later, I returned to Venezuela and participated in my first Yagé ceremony.

Ayahuasca is a powerful psychedelic brew traditionally used by Indigenous people throughout the Amazon basin. Within their cosmology, Ayahuasca brings healing to the body, mind, and spirit, allowing those who partake to tap into eternal wisdom and acquire a deep understanding of cosmic forces and jungle dynamics. It is always used within a ceremonial context and is facilitated using an intentional and sacred approach.

Leading up to the ceremony I was both excited and afraid. But as soon as I drank the traditional medicine, I began to experience the profound shift I was seeking. The ceremony took place over the course of two days, and for those two days I viscerally experienced nature as my teacher and began to feel more balance within myself. From that point on, I knew I wanted this ancient tradition to be part of my life.

After attending several more ceremonies in Venezuela over the next two years, I ended my relationship with my girlfriend and dropped out of university. During this time, I began participating in Ayahuasca ceremonies, which prompted a profound sense of inner healing in my relationship with my parents. I also began to feel a strong pull to travel to the Amazon, where these traditional ceremonies originated.

I spent five years living in the Amazon jungle in Peru, studying with an elder who has over fifty years of experience working with Ayahuasca and other sacred plants. I spent extensive periods of time in isolation ingesting different plant extracts, most of which are non-psychoactive. Through such periods of isolation, and by participating in repeated Ayahuasca ceremonies, I continued to heal old wounds, traumas and glean lessons that helped me make more sense of my varied life experiences.

Throughout the five years I spent in the Amazon, I made annual visits back to California, where I continued to explore other Indigenous healing practices, like sweat lodges and peyote ceremonies. The sweat lodge proved to be particularly powerful to me. Each time I participated in this ritual, I felt more energized and lighter in spirit. The peyote ceremonies were also transformative and beneficial to my process of healing. My connection with the element of fire was ignited during these ceremonies, which are centered around a fire burning constantly, from sunset to sunrise.

In my fourth year in the Amazon, I was offered a job at a healing retreat center, where I served as a translator and supported people process their Ayahuasca experiences. During this time, I learned a great deal about assisting and guiding people through intense spiritual healing journeys.

Since then, I have continued to study traditional Indigenous healing practices and facilitate them for others interested in healing their own wounds and traumas. The scope of this book comes from twelve years of personal inner-work aided by traditional Indigenous methods. The information I share is a direct result of these experiences and is meant for anyone interested in healing, growing, and letting go of the blockages or conditioning that prevent us from living a happy, successful, and fulfilled life. The lessons are universal and can be learned with, or without, the use of sacred plant medicines.

I hope you benefit from all that I am sharing.

Blessed journeys,

Alberto

December 21st, 2021

INTRODUCTION

We are living in a paradoxically bizarre time. Through incredible technological advancements, we are able to send people to the moon, map the cellular structures of our bodies, and virtually speak face-to-face with almost anyone on Earth. Yet we are facing a real existential threat. We are destroying our planet by exploiting our forests and minerals, contaminating our soils and waters, and letting the waste of our consumerist lifestyle pile up in landfills and on floating islands of trash in the ocean.

Where is the disconnect? If we apply a spiritual perspective to this insurmountable problem, the current state of the earth reflects how deeply wounded we humans are as a whole. Someone deeply rooted in self-love, integrity, and honesty wouldn't pollute and poison their home, water, lands and food supply. But people affected by their emotional traumas are unable to see clearly. They are at the mercy of their traumas, wounds and conditioning—by which I mean the parental, cultural, and societal beliefs passed down and unconsciously absorbed, which cause blockages and prevent personal growth.

Humans carry pain and suffering caused by our previous generations. From its foundation, our capitalist society has been founded in blood, pain, and suffering. Colonization, exploitation, slavery, and religious indoctrination have influenced almost every aspect of our lives today. Trace back five or six generations, and we are likely to find someone in our direct lineage who perpetrated, or was the victim of, major pain and suffering. Spiritually speaking, both parties—giver and receiver —of such violence are deeply wounded. Through the years, many descendants of families who played influential roles during colonial eras have continued to hold positions of power. Generation after generation, their emotional and spiritual traumas have been passed on. Hence, many people currently in positions of influence and power carry major unaddressed traumas. These people are making vital decisions about the future of our planet, and by extension, humanity as a whole. Yet wounded people who have not healed their traumas lack the clear vision necessary to make decisions affecting others. Especially under pressure, a person's true character is revealed, and if someone has unhealed wounds, it will quickly become apparent that they are unable to act with integrity. We have seen this play out dramatically as the Covid-19 pandemic has wreaked havoc throughout the world. Many global leaders have demonstrated that they are incapable of leading effectively.

The most common personal trauma is related to the relationship between parent and child. An unhealthy upbringing creates deep wounds and major trauma. If it's not addressed and healed, it will be carried through an entire lifetime, making the wounded person vulnerable to corruption, infidelity, and bigotry. The void created by the absence of a proper paternal or maternal figure, or by an unhealthy relationship with the parents, cannot be filled by anything but proper healing.

Thankfully, younger generations are increasingly engaged in ending generational trauma by exposing the damage it has caused to communities and natural environments. Teen climate activist Greta Thunberg is a great example of this trend. But Thunberg and many other young activists find themselves up against government officials and politicians who continue to pass laws that fail to protect the environment. These officials lack the necessary self-love to care for the planet. Instead, driven by capitalist ideals, they attempt to fill an inner void with money and luxury, unaware that their spiritual emptiness can be filled only by healing their traumas. Unfortunately, many world leaders do not prioritize the deep inner work of healing trauma, which cultivates the high moral virtues their positions require. Consequently, they lack the capacity for vision, foresight, and insight, qualities necessary to create a sustainable civilization. People in positions of power must engage in extensive inner work, or spiritual development, to perform their tasks with integrity, honesty, and responsibility.

However, we cannot blame only those in power for the state of our world. We, too, are responsible for allowing such leaders to hold power. Our own wounds and traumas have blurred our vision, preventing us from fully seeing the consequences of our choices. The capacity for such clear vision develops slowly, as we do inner work and nurture our spiritual selves. The deeper we connect with ourselves, the deeper we connect with the Universal Energy - Creator or God - which sustains all life.

From such inner space, we receive infallible guidance, allowing us to make better choices that return us to balance with ourselves and our home planet.

Fortunately, we have endless opportunities to receive the support we need to heal ourselves. In fact, never before in human history have the wisdom and tools for healing, growth, and spiritual development been so accessible to everyone. In ancient times, spiritual wisdom was heavily guarded and rarely shared. Now, we can access almost any self-help, religious, or spiritual book desired. Healing modalities such as yoga, meditation, and qigong are widely available. Traditional plant medicine ceremonies, which help us reconnect with ourselves and our Creator, are becoming increasingly accessible.

The only way to heal the human race and our planet is to heal each human individually. Our responsibility is to deal with our own emotional baggage. As we heal ourselves, the transition to taking better care of our planet will happen naturally and organically.

We must create a society which produces non-toxic waste that can be used to feed and replenish our soils; technology engineered with a high degree of recyclability; and transportation which absorbs excess carbon dioxide from the atmosphere. We need to create a society whose leaders voluntarily seek out sweat lodges, meditation retreats, vision quests, or the counsel of sacred plant medicines to rid themselves of negative traits and heal their wounds, traumas, and conditioning.

Within my lifetime, I hope to see humanity transition into a society that values such principles, understands the power of healing our own wounds, and cares deeply for the well-being of our planet. For that reason, my intention with this book is to inspire people and provide tools for spiritual development and healing. Incredible geniuses live among us, waiting for the moment to share their sustainable inventions, healing techniques, or ancient practices and make the world a better place. We have the capacity, technology, and means to change our consumerism into sustainability. Humanity can establish strong connections to both worlds, the material and the spiritual, for we are made of both. We just need to care for our material world sustainably and realize that our spiritual development must be a top priority.

FOLLOWING YOUR PATH: A LIFELONG JOURNEY

WE ALL DESIRE a life filled with love, abundance, and success. Who wouldn't want life to be enriching, purposeful, and fulfilling? We dream of what we wish to accomplish in this lifetime, yet we often sacrifice those dreams for routine and security. This makes sense, as we are constantly bombarded with information intended to manipulate us into finding happiness through consumerism. We lack role models who can show us how to live in harmony with our inner guidance. Even family and friends who influence us positively also pass along unhealthy habits and characteristics.

In order to live a life free from limiting beliefs, we need to put the necessary time and work into healing our wounds, conditioning and traumas. As we heal, learn, and grow, opportunities will inevitably arise to meet us on our path. We will begin to live more fulfilling lives, in which we are more connected to our true selves and all of creation. We will intimately feel the abundance of nature and realize that we are innately tied to the stars, planets, jungles, rivers, and oceans. And then we will feel in perfect balance with all of creation, a state that is currently beyond the ability of our minds to understand.

Spiritual evolution takes place during the course of a lifetime. It is not a trendy experience we can commit to for a weekend, expecting to return to our "normal" selves and lives afterwards. Whether we realize it or not, we embark on a spiritual path from before the moment we are born until the moment we let go of our bodies and journey into the unknown. But consciously awakening to this spiritual journey (which is accessible to everyone, not just spiritual gurus or teachers) allows us to make different choices that will bring change, healing, growth, and transformation into our daily lives.

Each person has an important purpose to accomplish within their lifetime. Most of the time, that purpose lies dormant under a layer of unresolved wounds, traumas, and conditioning. The energy of our traumas – the vibration of the emotions relating to the traumatic event - prevents us from aligning ourselves fully with our purpose. In choosing to work on our own healing, we awaken the awareness of our life's purpose.

This process takes time, work and focus. The lessons and the Universal Principles, described more fully in the following chapter, provide the rock-solid foundation that we need to become more aligned with our life's work. Just as a house needs a concrete foundation to withstand harsh weather, seasons, and time, we need the Universal Principles to create the solid foundation to expand, heal and grow. Without a solid foundation, our path will take us only so far before our work crumbles in front of our eyes. Because we lack spiritual structure, we will not be able to withstand the pressure of growth.

Remember, carbon requires copious amounts of pressure to develop into a diamond. In the same way, the pressure of our wounds, traumas, or conditioning creates the perfect, unique conditions we need to grow—and, eventually, become the diamonds we are meant to be. As challenges arise during this healing process, knowing how to apply each Universal Principle will aid us tremendously. (And those challenges will arise, I guarantee you.) As we heal, we'll face uncomfortable, even scary, aspects of ourselves. Yet in this place of discomfort, profound growth occurs. It is important to have patience with ourselves as we do this deep work. We cannot rush growth and healing. Hurrying the process may result in adverse effects, and we may be tempted to stop. If we take on more than we can handle, we may burn out and give up. But this is not a race, and there is no finish line. Following our spiritual path is a lifelong journey. And we may never fully feel like we've figured it all out.

Every situation we encounter demands our complete attention. The strength of our foundation is constantly tested. How well will we consciously choose to act according to our principles? If we react unconsciously, we only feed the patterns we want to heal. Hence, cultivating the Universal Principles will give us the proper tools we need to navigate the ebb and flow of life with ease and grace.

. . .

I like to think of life as a voyage on the ever-changing ocean, exposed to wind, waves, rain, and storms. I oversee my sailboat. I am constantly choosing how to adjust my sails (perspective and attention) and my ropes (Universal Principles) to whatever is happening in the ocean (life). If I have favorable winds, I'll open the sails fully to increase momentum in the direction that I am heading. If I encounter a storm (life challenges), I'll furl the sails until I can see a pathway through the storm. The ebb and flow of life calls for flexibility, adaptability, and a clear vision. Otherwise, we get lost in the storms of transformation.

Integrating the lessons outlined in this book will help us develop the capacity to achieve our goals. But integration is key. Unlike in formal Western studies, spiritual development cannot be attained just from reading a book (including this one) or obtaining a university degree. Only through direct experience can we develop our inner selves and gather the wisdom and lessons that reveal themselves as we learn to make different choices.

Following your spiritual path is a process of bringing unity to all aspects of your life, so you can live in unison with your whole being and in resonance with all creation. Your priorities —your job, choice of partner, diet, friends, location, and the areas in life that provide you with support—are all part of your spiritual path. Every aspect of yourself is connected. You can't compartmentalize your inner self. Remember, no one can do your inner work for you; just as you can't do someone else's for them. Like a farmer who carefully plows, weeds, and feeds the soil where he will plant crops, you, too, must carry out your inner work with care, attending to the Principles. Being aware of how you contribute to your daily experiences is crucial. After you have spent the proper time and attention developing the Universal Principles within yourself, harvest season will come, bringing juicy lessons and invaluable wisdom. Ultimately, you will be rewarded with a sense of profound freedom to live the life you have dreamed of and experience true and lasting love, filling your mind, body and soul.

CHAPTER I

LAYING DOWN THE FOUNDATION

"You can't build a great building on a weak foundation. You must have a solid foundation if you are going to have a strong super structure."

— Gordon B. Hinckley

OUR BELIEFS AND THE SUBCONSCIOUS PROGRAMING WE CARRY

WE NEED to explore the impact of our beliefs on our lives, behaviors, and experiences. They represent the most basic units of our consciousness. Each of our beliefs is firmly ingrained within our conscious and subconscious mind, dictating mental processes that influence our feelings and behavior, even without our awareness.

It may be helpful to think of our beliefs as the building blocks of our consciousness. When we set out to build a house, we need to properly lay out the foundation with the correct building blocks that will physically support the weight of the house. In the same way, we must consciously cultivate the proper set of beliefs that will support our spiritual development. In order to do this, we must first acknowledge the source of our current beliefs and begin letting go of those that hinder us in any way.

9

. . .

Many of the beliefs we hold are inherited from our parents, which makes sense, as parents are our first teachers. While some of what we inherit is positive, we also inherit our parents' fears and traumas. This is how generational trauma is passed down from parents to children through generations. If the beliefs are positive and help us grow, there is no need to change them; but if the beliefs are creating disturbances in our lives, we need to identify and alter them. Otherwise, beliefs generated from fear and trauma will direct our lives. Reprogramming our beliefs will enable us to stay grounded and centered when we face challenges, instead of being reactive.

It is also important to reprogram beliefs that may be limiting your full potential. For example, if you grew up in a household where you were told that you can earn money only through hard work, the only way you will make money is through hard work. You have been programmed this way. Other opportunities will not come to you. On the other hand, if you were told that you can become a person who follows and realizes your dreams, that programming will bring the necessary opportunities for you to fulfill your dreams. This parental programming applies to all areas of your life. Your friendships, romantic relationships, sense of self-worth, self-confidence, social views, understanding of gender roles, cultural dynamics, and more, are all influenced by these beliefs.

The process of unpacking limiting beliefs can be tricky, because most of our hindering beliefs lie deeply hidden within our subconscious mind, and we are so familiar with them that they

FROM WOUND TO WISDOM

are like water to a fish. We may also discover discrepancies among the beliefs, paradigms, or convictions which guide our lives. Recognizing such discrepancies is a good first step towards aligning our beliefs and eliminating a constant inner tug-of-war. One way to help organize and analyze conflicting paradigms is to list our priorities. The process of sorting out priorities helps reveal areas where our beliefs are not in alignment with the vision we have for our lives.

OUR WOUNDS, TRAUMAS, AND CONDITIONING

THE BELIEFS INGRAINED in us by our parents, culture, religion, and life experiences condition us to live a certain way. And when we don't consciously examine why we live this way, abiding by beliefs that we inherited, we cannot live up to our full potential. Likewise, unhealed wounds or traumas continue to hinder us long after the events that initially scarred us, which limits our potential. In the following chapters we will unpack how to release such conditioning, wounds, and traumas, so that we can free ourselves from unhealthy patterns and live our true purpose.

To better understand what I mean by conditioning, wounds, and trauma, I am including some definitions here. As mentioned earlier, conditioning includes all the inherited beliefs that influence, guide and control our lives. Emotional wounds are points of distress within ourselves caused by situations that bring emotional pain and suffering. Trauma is the psychological effect of an emotional wound on the mind. More often than not, we are all affected by conditioning, wounds, and traumas. Sometimes we battle with inherited beliefs that we want to discard, not connected with a specific trauma or wound. But when we do have wounds and traumas that need healing, we must address the limiting beliefs about ourselves that arise from experiencing such pain.

Most of our conditioning occurs during childhood, which is the time when we learn about the world, how to interact with people, what is acceptable, and what is not. As kids, we absorb information constantly by using our intuition, listening, seeing, and feeling; but we do not have the capacity to be fully aware of how deeply our parents' issues affect and condition us. We pick up on, and adopt, our parents' beliefs about money, social status, religion, relationships, political views, and much more. Such conditioning, while potentially limiting, is not necessarily traumatizing. It just teaches us to behave a certain way, vote for a particular political party, or have certain religious preferences. If we wish to change that programming, we need to determine what kind of belief we wish to replace it with and work diligently to bring forth the change.

If we have wounds from our childhood, they most probably spring from the dynamic we had with parents and family. Parents commonly have deep wounds themselves, resulting from interactions with their own parents. When they have children of their own, ocassionally they act from that wounded space. Most of the time, wounds from a parent-child relationship create strong behavioral patterning or conditioning, which is often perpetuated beyond childhood. For example, if a child is told that he or she is loved, but is spanked for doing something "wrong," the child becomes confused. From a child's point of view, the person they trust and love most is also a person who causes them pain. Such an experience creates an emotional wound and a trauma. If it only happens once, it may heal quickly. But if the abuse continues, the child begins to learn limiting and harmful beliefs, such as, "If you love me, you will abuse me." That belief may follow the child as they grow into adolescence and adulthood, unless a deep healing process takes place.

Without properly healing the wounds inflicted by our parents, we are set up to have a slew of emotional troubles in our relationships, particularly with intimate partners. Through my personal healing and experience in helping people going through their healing process, I have seen that the biggest part of healing is addressing wounds from parents. That's the main root of the dysfunction. Once we address the root, all the smaller tendrils (issues that develop from the main wound) begin to heal. Many common psychological conditions, like addictions, anxiety, or depression have their roots in unresolved childhood wounds, traumas, and conditioning.

If you can't immediately identify your wounds, your triggers may indicate which areas need attention and healing. For instance, you may feel angry, sad, or frustrated by an interaction with someone, but that person is not the sole source of your negative emotions. They merely triggered a wound you already had, which has gone unaddressed. By paying attention to your triggers, you can pinpoint internal areas that you have been neglecting or were unaware of.

As we examine each trigger, we strive to connect the emotional response and situation to the deeper wound within, initiating the healing of that wound. We will know that we have healed the wound once situations that previously triggered us no longer evoke such an emotional reaction.

The beauty of our wounds, conditioning, and traumas is that they carry lessons tailored specifically to each one of us. It is a rewarding process to move through the pain and suffering and to come out the other side with humbleness, gratitude, and powerful wisdom.

THE POWER OF A CHANGE IN PERSPECTIVE

WE ALL KNOW the analogy of the half-empty, half-full cup. Minds conditioned to see lack will look at the cup as half empty, whereas minds conditioned to see abundance will see the cup as half full. This change in perspective is quite simple, but as we will learn, the simplest things require work and time to accomplish. In fact, achieving anything that has real value requires these essential components.

I have come to see that life is the school of the soul. I firmly believe that our main purpose in life is to learn and grow, whether we are aware of it or not, in order to keep up with the momentum of an ever-expanding Universe. We are either expanding or contracting. Nothing in the Universe sits idle. Every aspect of creation is in constant flux and change. That's why our individual life paths constantly supply us with lessons uniquely tailored to our particular stage of spiritual growth.

Unless we are on the lookout for those lessons, we will miss valuable opportunities for spiritual development.

From this moment on, I invite you to commit yourself to a new way of seeing life: from the perspective of a constant learner, with the capacity to develop your consciousness and awareness. From this perspective, learning is our innate purpose, and we can begin creating a momentum of positivity within. We can see the value of the lessons that we are gathering, which will fill us with gratitude, transforming the mood of any spiritual development process.

The Universal Energy has the unique ability to teach us by "whispering" when we have a lesson to learn. If we are not paying attention, the intensity of the situations created for our learning begins to escalate, demanding our attention. And if we are still not getting it, the Universal Energy will find a way to make us stop everything, so we can listen and learn. I highly recommend listening to the subtle tugs from the Universal Energy, before it makes us pump the breaks full-stop, as that can be a painful experience. I have experienced this personally several times in my life, and it's taught me to pay closer attention to the subtleties of daily life.

A few years back, my actions were not in alignment with my path. The subtle cues came and went, while I ignored the lesson at hand. More emphatic signs came my way, to no avail, until I ended up in a car accident and a nine-month period of recovery. During this time, I was forced to reflect on my life choices and began to find great value in the lessons I was being taught: Always follow your intuition.

Just two years after the accident, I was supporting many people and doing deep inner work, when I failed again to see and listen to a major lesson being presented to me. That's when I contracted malaria, which reminded me once again to always listen to my intuition. While bedridden, I realized that I was feeling drained from overworking, and had been for some time. Yet I had not paid attention to that feeling. It took a malaria relapse and six months of recovery to cement that lesson in.

Our growth comes in cycles, and the level of intensity varies for everyone. The Universal Energy delivers the conditions that we need in order to learn and grow. For me, the accident and the malaria were amazing teachers. I found great value in the experiences, and I moved to a place of gratitude for all that had happened. The soft knocks of some are the hard knocks of others. Not everybody needs a car accident and malaria to learn a lesson. That's what I needed at that particular time in order to learn and grow. If you are paying close attention to your experiences, you will progress with ease and save yourself plenty of hassle and suffering.

I share these two incidents, for it is quite normal to fall back into old patterns, even as we heal ourselves of conditioning that is hindering us in some way. We are changing a pattern that has been repeatedly played out in our consciousness for quite some time. It takes work to reconfigure thought patterns and integrate new ways of thinking into our lives. This is only possible if we are paying close attention to our experiences and feelings. Feelings are of great value, as they alert us when something, whether physical or emotional, is out of alignment. In the following pages, I present a set of Universal Principles that can be integrated into daily life as we consciously remake ourselves and learn to gather wisdom from our lives.

THE POWER OF OUR ATTENTION
AND AWARENESS

OUR ATTENTION IS EXTREMELY VALUABLE, because we need it to accomplish anything. We need our attention to set alarms to wake up in the morning, to perform our jobs, to be present in conversations with loved ones, to enjoy the movie we are watching, to study for our classes, and so forth. Without properly paying attention, we can't accomplish anything with satisfactory results.

And yet, we are living in a world that is trying its best to distract us. Never before has there been so much competition to capture our attention. Every day we are bombarded by advertisements trying to sell us ideas, products, services, etc. As we buy into these distractions, our power to live intentionally dissipates.

. . .

In our spiritual development our attention is of utmost importance, since it is only by paying attention to our lives that we will be able to learn from our experiences. If merely old age made us wise, every old person would possess powerful wisdom to share. In reality, only people who have taken the time to attentively develop themselves carry the valuable wisdom that can help us make better choices and improve the quality of our lives.

We need our full attention to be present with our experiences, so we can see what is happening in our lives. The processes involved in spiritual development do not work in linear ways. They come in cycles, each impacting different areas of our inner selves in need of further development. With the proper attention to these cycles over time, we are able to make connections between our lived experiences and specific areas in which we need spiritual development. By connecting the lessons' common denominators, we can start transforming the lessons into wisdom.

Awareness is an aspect of our attention. If we are paying attention to what is happening around us, we become aware of it. We need both awareness and attention to be present with our spiritual development.

Since we cannot separate our spiritual development from other parts of our lives, with the proper attention and awareness we will develop the capacity to identify lessons as we are immersed in our day-to-day lives. Lessons come from the least expected places or situations; therefore, we must remain open to seeing everyone and every situation as an opportunity to learn. This perspective proves most challenging when we are forced to deal with people or situations that trigger us, that touch our wounds, and remind us of our traumas.

But what matters in our personal inner work is action. What do we do with the awareness we have? How do we carry ourselves within the frame of our awareness? Do we put our awareness on a shelf, along with the rest of our books, to display? Or do we get it dirty, like the shovel we use to plant our veggies? We can think, theorize, philosophize, or conceptualize; but action materializes our awareness. For example, we can be aware that a certain behavior is unhealthy. However, unless we take steps to change it, awareness alone will not change the pattern.

I see awareness as the ability to adapt to changes gracefully. By possessing this ability, we can meet changes in our environment with true awareness, accompanied by the proper action, allowing us to adapt to new situations with grace. Like water in a river that finds its path, regardless of obstacles along the way, awareness gives direction to our actions, transmitting our purpose to the Universal Energy.

The process of spiritual development requires the capacity to be aware of what is happening within ourselves, and around us. As we work through these internal processes, we will be confronted with external challenges, which are opportunities to put into practice what we are learning. Awareness of the aspect of our inner selves we're working on, and attention to the situations we are attracting, allow us to see correlations between our inner and outer worlds. It is important to gather the lessons from this newfound awareness.

As we will come to see, attention and awareness represent the bow of our sailboat. By paying attention and being aware of where the wind is coming from, and how it is behaving (aspects of our inner selves and what is around us energetically), we can make appropriate adjustments to the direction of our boat and adjust our sails (decisions) accordingly, in order to continue moving forward in our journey of self-development.

THE POWER OF OUR CHOICES

Now that we know the value of our attention and awareness, we can explore why our choices carry such weight on our path of spiritual development. Our choices help determine what is brought into our lives by the Universal Energy, just as they can also let the Universal Energy know what we don't want in our mental, emotional, and physical space. With each choice we make, our beliefs, principles, and conditioning will help us grow, expand, and transform, or reinforce hindering beliefs, wounds, or traumas.

As we continue our spiritual path, we must constantly make choices that are in alignment with our development. Otherwise, we will be sending mixed signals to the Universal Energy. Keep in mind that our choices determine what the Universal Energy brings into our lives. It provides us with more of what we are choosing, whether those choices are made consciously or unconsciously. We must be vigilant in determining the emotional and mental space from which we make our choices. Each one must align with our principles, priorities, and the direction we are heading in our lives.

The Universal Energy reads actions more strongly than words. For example, if you know that certain foods are detrimental to your health, but you keep eating them, you send a message to the Universal Energy that you lack self-love (you are hurting yourself), and commitment (you're not following through); you also lack awareness of the consequences of your actions. The Universal Energy will provide you with situations that match your actions, whether they are positive or negative.

Spiritually speaking, energy is a non-physical force, or essence, that binds the universe together. Everything in the universe is composed of energy vibrating at a certain frequency, and energies that vibrate at the same frequencies attract each other. Since our individual energy is composed of the vibrating energy of our thoughts, deeds, wounds, traumas, and conditioning, we will attract the whole palette of energies into our life experience. As I explained earlier, through attention, awareness, and an openness to learning, we can consciously choose which kinds of energies we invite into our mental, physical and emotional space—and which kinds we will not tolerate.

When we make a choice, we commit to a flow of situations that will carry us until we gather its lessons. Each choice opens a process of growth. Some processes are short, and in a matter of days we will gather their lessons. Some processes will take longer, and we will need a few months, or even a period of years, to absorb their lessons. Our choices are the medium through which our spiritual growth is tested.

Each choice we make inherently expresses our priorities, commitment, self-love, integrity, honesty, responsibility, perspective, attention, and awareness. In the process of making a choice, we go through all these aspects of our inner selves. If we are not clear, or if we are still making decisions based on old conditioning and hindering beliefs, we will make choices from a place of disempowerment. These choices will be guided by aspects of ourselves that we wish to overcome, and choices made under such influences will cause great confusion. In order to move forward in our spiritual development and experience growth, the choices we make must come from a grounded and Heart-Centered space.

The Heart-Center is the space within us that is always connected to the Universal Energy, and it's the source of our intuition. We are all connected to all parts of creation. However, the effects of our wounds, conditioning, or traumas can cloud that connection. Consequently, it becomes harder to listen to what our Heart-Center is telling us. The choices we make that inspire growth help us strengthen the connection to our Heart-Center.

Our awareness while making choices is of great importance. We are letting the Universal Energy know what we want—and what we don't want. We must clearly understand our priorities, commitment, and focus. Remember, to move forward in your spiritual path, your commitment to inner work must be in your top five priorities, along with food, shelter, love, and work. Otherwise, you are telling the Universal Energy that your spiritual development is a secondary priority, which will stagnate and kill any momentum you might have developed.

The power of our choices also helps us develop healthy boundaries, which are necessary to protect ourselves from unhealthy relationships. With the proper choices, we can create and maintain healthy relationships, and also end relationships when they become unhealthy. When we choose to say no to abuse, manipulation, or lies, we are sending a powerful message out into the Universal Energy. Depending on the level of our development, we must assert ourselves by saying "No" until we can identify the hindering conditioning. In the same way, when we say "Yes" to a healthy relationship, we ask the Universal Energy to bring more healthy relationships.

It is necessary to let go of unhealthy friendships and intimate relationships so we can open physical and emotional space within our lives for new, healthy ones to arise. Do not let people that you care for mistreat, manipulate, or abuse you without making the choice to speak up for yourself. Express what you need to say in a respectful way. Otherwise, you are allowing the mistreatment to go on, and the Universal Energy will read and reciprocate it. If we don't choose wisely in our relationships, we compromise our inner work and our integrity.

INTRODUCTION TO THE UNIVERSAL PRINCIPLES

THE UNIVERSAL PRINCIPLES that I am about to present are quite simple, but I urge you not to underestimate the power behind them. Each Principle represents an individual thread. When we weave these Principles together, they form a beautiful, tight, strong rope, exponentially stronger than its individual threads. In the same way, as we cultivate these Principles within, we are weaving an enormous power that we can wield in our processes of spiritual development.

The rope we weave by cultivating these Principles within allows us to control the sails of our boat. Without ropes, a sailboat is at the mercy of wind and storm. Similarly, without having cultivated these Principles within, we can't properly navigate the flow of challenges that we are attracting when we commit to our spiritual development.

As you will soon see, these Universal Principles have been used by many teachers, preachers, and sages from all walks of life and religions. The beauty of these Principles and lessons is their utility to all people, regardless of religious or cultural backgrounds, because they invite you to be your own teacher. I can promise that once you begin this journey, there is no turning back, and the rewards are great. Committing ourselves to our spiritual development allows us to live the life we dream.

THE FIRST PRINCIPLE: COMMITMENT

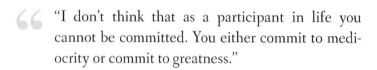

"I don't think that as a participant in life you cannot be committed. You either commit to mediocrity or commit to greatness."

—Les Brown

It is imperative to develop a high degree of commitment to our spiritual path, no matter what we find along the way. When we say, "Yes, I want to heal my wounds and work through my traumas and conditioning," we are asking the Universal Energy to start the flow of situations that will help us heal and grow. However, healthy challenges are bound to arise, because it is only through direct experience that we can heal and grow. Don't worry. Not every aspect of our inner selves needs a heavy challenge; only the most stubborn areas call forth drastic measures from the Universal Energy. At times, I have found myself thinking, "I am dealing with *this* again?" But the commitment I made to myself and my spiritual growth helps me carry on when my patience grows thin.

When we commit to our spiritual growth, we make our inner work a top priority. Focused and attentive, we willingly do what it takes to move through the processes of spiritual development. We need not put life on hold for months at a time, but if something discomforting happens at home or at work, we must take the time to listen to our feelings and emotions, processing the event before moving on to the next task. We all have busy lives these days, but when we sense an inner disturbance or conflict, it is important to make time to reflect. If we don't allow ourselves time to process our experiences, they pile up, and a big mess will be waiting for us next time we want to do inner work. It is easier to clean up regularly than to do a major cleanup at the end of the year.

Oftentimes, the Universal Energy forces us to face increasingly difficult challenges, in order to push us beyond our comfort zone, so we can continue to grow. Our commitment to our spiritual growth is tested in these moments. Yet I assure you that standing strong will help you face your biggest fears and navigate your way through immense struggle, even if there is seemingly no exit in sight.

As we continue to strengthen our commitment to our spiritual growth, we will bring that quality to relationships with family, friends, and loved ones, treating them with more dedication and care.

Incredible and previously unseen opportunities will also unveil themselves, the more we commit to staying on our spiritual path. The mind is often too limited to grasp these infinite possibilities. As we commit to listening to our intuition and the wisdom of our Heart-Center (which often defies all logic), we come to see how situations, energies and people are linked together, guided by a higher power.

Things don't happen just by chance. The unseen energy that binds creation together clusters similar energy frequencies. Hence, our commitment to spiritual development acts as a magnet, attracting what we need.

THE THREE ELEMENTS OF COMMITMENT: CONSISTENCY, PERSEVERANCE AND SELF-DISCIPLINE

THE THREE ASPECTS of commitment are consistency, perseverance and self-discipline. All are equally important. Take one away, and they all crumble. Consistency, perseverance, and self-discipline can be thought of as the legs of a tripod, helping support the structure of our commitment. Hence, we need proper time and drive to cultivate these inner qualities before we can rely on the power of our commitment. Without them, our minds will find any available loophole to escape commitment.

Consistency is necessary in order to create positive momentum in our spiritual development. If we lack consistency, we send mixed messages out into the Universal Energy, which will ultimately hinder us. Lack of consistency actually creates more work for us, because without it, we will need to repeat processes of spiritual development. For example, if you take a class and drop out, you must retake the whole class, and redo all the homework, in order to get full credit. It works the same way in our self-development. Maintaining consistent habits aids us in staying focused on our goals and develops integrity, which then permeates all aspects of our lives.

Perseverance is also critical as we continue along our spiritual journey. If we quit the moment we feel challenged, we stifle any potential for growth. Imagine a baby learning to walk. They fall down over and over, but the incredible perseverance they are blessed with allows them to master the art of walking. You don't hear a baby saying, "I wish learning to walk was easier," or "I don't know if I can stand up, if I fall again," or "Could somebody do the walking for me?" We need this quality as adults, in order to overcome the difficulties we all encounter, especially as we cultivate our inner power.

Practicing self-discipline is also critical to developing a strong commitment. We need self-discipline to wake up in the morning and arrive on time for jobs, classes, or appointments. We need self-discipline to perform tasks at home and at work. In the same way, we need to cultivate self-discipline when addressing our inner work. There is no spiritual police force that will come and make sure you are doing your inner work. As we sow our seeds, we shall harvest our food. The amount of work we put into our inner work correlates to the amount of growth we experience.

I learned about commitment through my love of surfing. The ocean has been an integral part of my life since I was a little kid.

I have always had a fascination with its wildness, expansiveness, and presence. My parents, on the other hand, thought surfing was dangerous. It took some years for me to convince them to buy me my first surfboard. Eventually, my perseverance paid off, and I learned that if I wanted something, I had to be determined to get it. I was eleven years old.

As I grew older, I made a commitment to myself that I would live to surf. I was not into competitions and sponsorships, but I loved the concept of soul surfing and exploring coastlines in foreign countries to find waves. I got a job at a travel agency, and with much perseverance, saved enough money to fund my first trip to Central America. A year later, with the help of my parents, I moved to the Canary Islands in Spain. I surfed every day for the next two years and committed to a physical training program of intensive biking and paddling while working and saving money to go to my next dream surf destination, Indonesia. During this time, I started to see the value of self-discipline, perseverance, and consistency. I got in the best physical shape of my life. Even though I was not doing spiritual development work at the time, this experience planted seeds that I later used when I was going through months of isolation in the Amazon jungle.

I was halfway through my training program when the 2004 earthquake and tsunami devastated Indonesia. Suddenly, I had to change my plans. I decided to go to Mexico, which hosts some of the world's most powerful waves. Surfing in Mexico demanded a new mindset. You had to believe fully in yourself. There was no room for hesitation. Even though the beach where I surfed had a sandy bottom, swimmers had drowned there, and a surfer had died, on a big day. The consequences of engaging with the ocean were real. While the size and power of the waves intimidated me at first, I was attracted to them, as well. In order to surf those big powerful waves, I had to be committed 100 percent. I had to persevere as I paddled out against strong currents and breaking surf. I had to be consistent about getting enough rest in order to conserve all my vitality for surfing. And I had to practice self-discipline to refrain from getting distracted by the constant lure of parties. Any time that I did not abide by these self-imposed rules, I paid the consequences in the water. Over the years, I have found myself drawing from the power I cultivated during the six months I surfed those waves with unwavering commitment.

Exercise

The easiest way to cultivate our commitment is through a regimen of physical exercise. Caring for our bodies is essential. Movement is necessary to maintain a healthy body. When we commit to a regimen of physical exercises, we cultivate our consistency, perseverance, and self-discipline. I cannot tell you which exercises fit your needs, because we all have different capabilities and limitations. You need to determine what kind of exercise is right for you, and work towards a goal beyond your current capabilities. The length and frequency of your commitment is also critical. A regimen with a minimum frequency of three times per week, for at least six months, will demonstrate what commitment, perseverance, consistency and self-discipline can bring into our lives.

THE SECOND PRINCIPLE: INTEGRITY

 "Whoever is careless with the truth in small matters cannot be trusted with important matters."

— Albert Einstein

Integrity plays a major role in expanding our consciousness. In simple terms, integrity demands that we "do as we say, and say as we do," with an awareness of the consequences of our actions. Being honest and maintaining strong moral principles provides the necessary strong foundation to navigate life's constant tests.

Cultivating inner integrity will prove to be priceless. When we lack integrity, we lack the proper foundation to pursue our deep inner work. As the "transformative hurricane season" hits our inner house built atop sand, everything will crumble, leaving us to start our inner work again from the beginning. Hopefully, we will gather some lessons in the process.

The easiest way to measure our integrity is by asking the question, "Am I living up to my word?" There was a time when someone's word was more valuable than any document. Long gone are those days. Since integrity is so crucial for inner work, before committing to anything, take the time to contemplate the proposition and determine if you can truly commit to it. Instead of agreeing right away in order to please people, even your friends, say you are going to think about it before you make any promises. If the proposition is in alignment with your priorities and commitments, move forward; otherwise, respectfully decline.

Cultivating integrity within takes attention and work, just as it does to grow plants and harvest food. In the same way, with the proper attention, consistency, and perseverance, we will gather the benefits of integrity. But first, we must commit to acting with integrity in all aspects of our lives. This process will also shed light on discrepancies within ourselves. As we examine these discrepancies, we are realigning our priorities and shedding unhealthy habits and beliefs. This process generates incredible momentum in our growth. Our relationships with others also improve naturally as we cultivate integrity within. It does not work the other way around. Integrity towards others, but not with ourselves, reveals a major imbalance which must be addressed right away. The more we live with integrity, the more we develop self-love and self-confidence. This generates a positive current, which attracts further positivity into our lives.

Integrity calls forth a deep inner awareness to guide us towards developing our full potential. The long and winding path of spiritual development greatly tests our beliefs, concepts, and conditioning. Inevitably, this journey exposes areas of weakness. It is an uncomfortable, and sometimes painful process that requires high levels of integrity. Without it, we will not be able to work on our weaknesses and pass the tests with grace. Remember, the tests and challenges placed along our path by the Universal Energy are but steppingstones to help us heal and transform into the jewels we truly are.

I began to see deeper into the meaning of integrity during my first trip to the Amazon, where I planned to learn about the ancient Amazonian tradition of ceremonial Ayahuasca. Prior to heading to the Amazon, I had not used cannabis for more than a year. I had intentionally stopped using it, knowing it was just a means to numb the residual pain I felt from unresolved childhood wounds. But upon arriving in the Peruvian jungle city of Iquitos, I started using it again. I discovered that my soon-to-be mentor and Ayahuasca facilitator, Jose, used it himself. For the next two years, whenever I emerged from periods of deep isolation in the Amazon, where I was learning about Ayahuasca, I began using cannabis again.

When my bank account dried, Jose suggested that I return to California and work on a cannabis farm. I spent three months in Humboldt County helping run the farm, all the while deepening my cannabis habit. At the time, I didn't see anything wrong with what I was doing. The money I was making would sustain me for nine months in the Amazon, where living was cheap. After those nine months, I returned to work in Humboldt County again, this time earning enough to sustain me for several years in the Amazon.

At first, I didn't realize that I was earning money from an industry that perpetuates addiction, instead of bringing healing to others. When I came to this realization, I decided that I couldn't dabble in both worlds at the same time—one promoting growth and healing, the other promoting addiction. As I got clear with my priorities and healed my cannabis habit, I was offered a job in the Amazon at an Ayahuasca retreat center. I worked as a translator and supported participants during ceremonies. It was then that I started to feel completely in alignment, because I was acting with integrity and earning money in a way that was in accordance with my life path. The Universal Energy always provides in amazing ways when we are in alignment with our principles and following the guidance of our Heart-Center.

Exercise

One of the best ways to start cultivating integrity is by making sure your beliefs are in alignment. To determine your beliefs, it is helpful to put them on paper. Decide on a topic you wish to reflect on, and write it at the top of a page. Then start writing the first thing that comes into your mind about that topic. DO NOT analyze what you are writing. Doing so will block the flow of beliefs from your subconscious mind. Topics you wish to explore might include money, employment, home, family, friendships, romantic relationships, sex, creativity, and beliefs about yourself, love, communication, religion, and spirituality. Feel free to pursue topics that resonate with you.

After you have written down all the beliefs you carry about one topic, move on to the next. Take your time with each topic, allowing your subconscious beliefs to arise. Once you have gone through all the topics, you will be able to compare your beliefs and discover which ones are contradictory. For example, a person may desire deep, meaningful friendships. But because they have been repeatedly hurt by friends, they subconsciously believe that all friendships are hurtful. Comparing your beliefs on different topics allows you to learn which beliefs need to change, so that you can develop a deeper integrity with yourself. This initial assessment creates a map of your beliefs. Read through the book and once you reach the section on affirmations in the Appendix, you will be able to consciously reprogram your beliefs. This exercise will expose the areas of yourself that need attention, and the affirmations will help heal and strengthen them.

To cultivate a different aspect of integrity, try the exercise of "Doing as you say, and saying as you do." There is no allowance for white or little lies on this path. Start by committing for one day to do as you say, and say as you do, at every moment—with yourself and others. If it is hard, give yourself a couple of days of rest, and commit again for one day. Slowly build up to two days. As you get more comfortable, keep adding days, until it becomes your way of being. If it is easy, continue with your commitment to being honest with yourself and others until it becomes your living standard.

THE THIRD PRINCIPLE: RESPECT

 "Respect for ourselves guides our morals; respect for others guides our manners."

—Laurence Stone

Respect and integrity create a powerful synergy, as they are intimately tied. By acting with integrity, we show respect for ourselves. And cultivating deep respect for ourselves is paramount to our spiritual development.

Respect for our feelings, wishes, rights, abilities, and achievements, and those of others, prompts us to listen to our inner guidance and adjust our choices so they are in tune with our intuition. If we are feeling emotional, we need to create a safe physical space to deal with our emotions. If we are feeling tired and depleted, we need to create time and the environment for us to replenish. If we need to express ourselves, we will do it in a respectful way for all parties involved. As we cultivate respect for ourselves, we will be able to do the same for others. Then we will experience how the respect we give to ourselves is reciprocated by the Universal Energy.

We develop respect for ourselves by knowing our own worth. We are all valuable, each with a unique path here on Earth and a unique skill set waiting to come forth for the betterment of humanity. If you don't feel you have much value, make a list of your strengths. This will help you value and appreciate your inner qualities and increase your level of self-respect. Allowing others to overstep your boundaries is one indicator that you don't fully value yourself. On the flip side, if you assign too much value to yourself, you may overstep the boundaries of others. Check in with yourself to identify areas that may need balance. Balance will develop naturally as you consistently demonstrate respect for yourself and others in all situations.

As we develop our own self-value and worth, we will not tolerate, nor allow, certain situations or people in our lives. Naturally, as we continue to grow more in alignment with our inner guidance, we find ourselves letting go of behaviors, people, and places that don't resonate with our newfound awareness. As we relinquish these old aspects, we create mental and emotional space to form a new relationship with ourselves. Simultaneously, we will have more space in our lives to develop new, beautiful friendships, new ways to relate with others in general, and new activities in alignment with our freshly developed awareness.

I had quite a bumpy road in the process of developing self-respect. I was raised in a home where spanking was the primary form of discipline. I believe I was only four years old when I got my first spanking. The memory is still there. I was utterly heartbroken. My mom, whom I loved deeply, spanked me for reasons I can't remember, and I completely lost trust in her. I could not understand how the person who loved me, and was supposed to protect me, hit me. That action imprinted an inner conditioning that took me thirty-two years to overcome. Repeated spankings throughout my childhood cemented the idea that love and abuse are intertwined. Consequently, when I got into a relationship with my first girlfriend, I lost myself in the relationship, seeking her love constantly, all the while being manipulated and abused by her. These types of problems in my romantic relationships continued for quite some time.

One of the most tumultuous and painful times of my life occurred during my four-year marriage. My wife and I were constantly at war with each other. This relationship was eye-opening, because I recognized traits of my mother in her, which frightened and angered me. I was still angry at my mom, and to realize that I had married a younger version of her made me upset with my wife—and with myself. Towards the end of our fourth year of marriage, I had had enough and asked for a divorce. The divorce was slow and painful, but it started the process of developing deeper self- respect. It took two more long-term relationships, and four years of learning about traditional healing in the Amazon, for me to connect all these experiences and trace them back to the wound with my mom. But when I did, it was an incredible moment. I felt like a weight was lifted from me. Suddenly, I felt I had more autonomy, and a deep self-respect was generated within me.

After this realization, I decided to remain single for several years. I was finally out of the jungle, next to the ocean again, and started developing my healing practice, which meant plenty of work. When I eventually started to crave female companionship again, I consulted with my Reiki teacher, who encouraged me to start dating. But early in my next relationship, I began to see old patterns of abuse emerging, and I decided to break up with my girlfriend. In that process, I defined the qualities that I needed my future partner to embody.

Exercise

In order to evaluate your level of self-respect, you must develop a keen awareness of the messages you send yourself through words and actions. For three days, write down all the self-talk that goes through your mind. Include opinions and beliefs about yourself. You may also want to list certain actions or behaviors that send a particular message about your sense of self-worth. The point of this exercise is to shine a light on areas of yourself where you lack self-respect. Having done this, you can begin the process of transforming those opinions and behaviors from negative to positive. This sort of transformation and "reframing" of negative thought patterns requires deep self-reflection. You will need to examine how those beliefs were formed, and how they have been cemented into your daily life. Keep a record of all your answers, because in chapters II and III of this book you will use them to continue in your journey of self-exploration.

THE FOURTH PRINCIPLE: HONESTY

 "Honesty is the first chapter in the book of wisdom."

— Thomas Jefferson

To cultivate a rock-solid inner foundation, we must be honest. We must be truthful and sincere to ensure that our actions are free from ill-intention. If we lie to ourselves on this path of self-development, we are only hindering ourselves from progressing on the journey. Being honest with ourselves means staying committed to seeing all our actions and shortcomings with a non-judgmental eye, and being open to identifying areas within ourselves that we need to work on.

. . .

Remember, whatever we refuse to look at now will be placed in our path repeatedly. If we don't gather the lessons from a specific situation, we will be confronted in the future with a similar one, providing us another opportunity to learn what we failed to absorb earlier. As I shared before, we came into this life to learn and grow. Therefore, we can see each situation as an opportunity given by the Universal Energy to expand and develop, to reach our greatest potential. From this perspective, we can see that unless we are completely honest with ourselves, we can fall victim to our own lies, until we once again abide by the core Principles. If we find ourselves lying, we should ask ourselves why. Are we ashamed of something we did, or something that happened to us? We must be able to tell our life story without lies or regrets, because it has shaped us into who we are today.

I learned this during my own self-healing journey. While I thought I had healed my childhood wounds, which stemmed mostly from my relationship with my mother, the Universal Energy kept showing me I had more work to do. In every romantic relationship, the same unhealthy patterns with women emerged; but I refused to see them, because I was not being honest with myself. Once I started to be completely honest with myself, I was able to start recognizing these unhealthy patterns and begin looking for signs of healing.

Exercise

The simplest way to cultivate honesty with ourselves is to be completely free of self-deceit. We all have inner dialogues that we use to process our experiences. It is quite easy to tell ourselves "white lies" that won't harm anyone. But those white lies actually do a great deal of harm. Every time we lie to ourselves, we turn a blind eye to an aspect of ourselves that needs attention. In order to cultivate honesty, we must be truthful about what is happening in our inner world. If we are triggered by someone's action, we must acknowledge it, rather than lying to ourselves by saying that the event made no impact. When we acknowledge our triggers, the door opens to a deeper process of self-inquiry. But this happens only when we are honest and truthful with ourselves. For this exercise, go through the day without telling any lies. First commit to one day, then to two, and so forth, until all self-deceit is stopped. Take the needed time to move through this exercise.

THE FIFTH PRINCIPLE: COMPASSION

 "Instead of putting others in their place, put yourself in their place."

— Amish Proverb

Developing compassion for others starts with developing compassion for ourselves. In this path of inner work, we are bound to make mistakes. It is part of the journey to get ourselves all tangled up in the blackberries (otherwise known as our mistakes). These mistakes hurt, and may even make us cry or bleed. But the pain will only be exacerbated if we cannot refrain from being harsh, hurtful, or abusive towards ourselves while learning from our mistakes. Having compassion for ourselves requires that we release these judgmental patterns, so we can continue our transformational process. The more we can be loving, patient, and compassionate with ourselves, the easier it will be to stand up every time we fall.

Compassion acknowledges our difficulties and encourages us to be responsible for our experiences. It empowers us to make changes in our life, so we don't make the same mistakes in the future. Eventually, as we learn to have compassion for ourselves, we are able to have compassion for others and support them in their own self-development journeys. However, showing compassion should not be confused with doing the work for others. For example, we may find ourselves in situations where loved ones are about to make a huge mistake. Sometimes it is necessary to let them make the mistake, and allow them to go through the process of experiencing adversity, in order for them to grow. Trying to help them fix their situations does not demonstrate compassion. Instead, it encourages dependency. Compassion for others requires us to empower them to draw upon their own inner strength to work through difficult situations.

True compassion is like the morning dew on a flower, it requires certain conditions. Cultivating principles such as commitment, integrity, respect and honesty helps create the right conditions for us to act compassionately with ourselves and others. As we combine these principles, they help us develop a more centered, connected, and balanced approach to life. And in the process, we open new levels of self-love, appreciation, and understanding, all of which increase the momentum of our growth.

· · ·

Throughout my life, I have held myself to high standards. To my passions, I give all my attention and time. But this has also meant that I've been hard on myself, particularly as I was growing up. Whenever I made a mistake, I was angry with myself. It wasn't until I spent two months in isolation in the Amazon that I started to understand what it meant to have compassion for myself. During that period of isolation, I did not interact with anyone, except a friend who brought me supplies once a week. The experience of complete solitude brought my wounds and conditioning to the surface. My many mistakes in life floated through my consciousness. At first, it was hard to sit with all of this. But after ten days on a limited diet, I lacked the physical strength to be hard on myself. Instead, I was guided to find the value in my mistakes. That was a turning point. As I contemplated each mistake, eventually a valuable lesson from it would emerge. Having the time and space to be alone allowed me to see those lessons as jewels. The moment I discovered each one, my heart softened, transforming the anger about my shortcomings into gratitude for the lessons, and compassion for myself. Towards the end of those two months in isolation, I felt a weight lifted from my heart. From that moment forward, I gave myself more love, and less punishment, for the mistakes I made. In doing so, I began to have more compassion for others, as well.

Exercise

Contemplate the moments in your life when you feel you have made a mistake. What feelings are attached to those mistakes? Write down the mistake with its accompanying feelings. Now, ask yourself, "What did I learn from my mistake?" Once you find a lesson, how do you feel? Take your time to contemplate each mistake, starting with ones that seem minor or insignificant. Gradually, challenge yourself to reflect on more serious mistakes that you regret making. The gradual progression will help you to cultivate appreciation and gratitude towards your mistakes and compassion for yourself. By the time you get to the more serious mistakes, you will have a deeper foundation of compassion, allowing you to see beyond the regret and into its everlasting wisdom.

THE SIXTH PRINCIPLE: COURAGE

 "You cannot swim for new horizons until you have
the courage to lose sight of the shore."

— William Faulkner

Courage is the wind that blows in our sails when we begin to
follow the compass of our Heart-Center. Through highs and
lows, through winter and summer, through storms and calm,
courage is exercised and strengthened as we follow the guidance of our Heart-Center.

Following our Heart-Center guidance is one of the most
courageous things we can do as we foster our spiritual development. We need courage to overcome our fears, so we can follow

our calling, live our dreams, and share our gifts and skills with the world. But overcoming our fears does not happen overnight. Courage is like a muscle—the more we exercise it, the stronger it gets. Facing small fears one at a time is a good way to begin working out our bravery muscle. With each small act of bravery, we are able to successfully lift more weight with increasing grace. In the process, we break unhealthy fear-based patterns that have stunted our growth. But in order to reach that point, we must also have the courage to examine blockages that may be perpetuating a fear-based mentality. These blockages are usually caused by past traumas, wounds, and limiting beliefs acquired throughout our lives.

When we commit ourselves to compassionately exploring and healing these blockages, we begin to experience synchronicities that support us in fulfilling our true purpose. It is important to face our fears, as they hold in place old patterns which stunt our growth and slow the healing of our wounds, conditioning, and traumas. Facing our fears allows us to break the ice of these patterns and develop our courage.

As a surfer, I have always had an attraction to adrenaline and pushing my limits, which inherently has cultivated my courage. Dealing with the immensity of the ocean, the waves, the currents, and the potential risks, has shaped that inner desire to step out of my comfort zone. But I didn't tackle big surf right away. I grew up surfing small waves in a sheltered Caribbean Sea. Through physical training, I built a deeper level of trust in my capabilities and slowly started going out in bigger surf. This gradual approach allowed me to learn how the ocean changes when the waves get bigger, and how the currents within the surf break shift. In time, I learned to navigate these ever-changing conditions with a sense of calm. I have applied this same approach to my process of spiritual development. As I addressed more superficial challenges, I began to understand the inner work process. I came to perceive the importance of not getting carried away by emotions, and how time and emotional space are necessary for healing to occur without pressure. Throughout this process I built trust in my capabilities, which gave me the confidence to tackle my bigger wounds.

Exercise

The first step to building more courage is to do something just outside your comfort zone. This can be as simple as building your confidence in public speaking by giving a presentation to a group of friends. (Keep in mind that you will need to prepare your presentation in order to build trust in your capabilities.) Pick an activity that excites you and makes you feel butterflies in your stomach. Gradually, demand more of yourself. If you started with a presentation for five friends, invite ten to the next one. To the following one, invite twenty. This progression will prepare you for your first public speaking appearance in front of strangers, and the gradual approach can be applied to any activity. After you have gone through a full cycle of reaching a goal well beyond your comfort zone, start addressing other fears in the same way.

THE SEVENTH PRINCIPLE: PATIENCE

 "Patience is not only the ability to wait, it is how we behave while we are waiting"

— Joyce Meyer

Patience is perhaps the most obvious, yet the most underestimated, of the Principles. It is imperative to have patience with ourselves as we begin our inner work. Facing and overcoming our fears and healing our wounds, conditioning, or traumas may take days, weeks, months, years, decades, or a lifetime. No matter how long it takes to experience such evolution in our personal growth, we must practice staying calm and accepting without complaining about any delays or annoyances that arise. Complaining about the process helps maintain the pattern, wound, or fear we wish to heal and transform.

. . .

Two variables influence the length of our inner development processes. The first is our ability to recognize the lessons; the second is our ability to integrate them into our lives. As we cultivate inner patience, we accept with more ease and grace the difficulties and challenges that arise in our path. Complaining about our current state of development doesn't help us move forward. In fact, it promotes a victim mentality, diminishing our inner-power and making it more difficult to see and integrate the lessons we are being offered.

Anytime I have tried to speed up the processes involved in my spiritual development, it does not pan out well. I've learned that when I am too focused on what I need to do in the future, I miss the steps I need to take in the present. As I focus more on my present and harvest its lessons, my next step becomes evident. If I don't integrate the lessons, though, the next step is unreachable.

Practicing patience also requires us to look at the most sensitive aspects of ourselves. Such a task is not easy; it takes effort and attention to detail. As we patiently go through our processes of inner development, we learn to see how they work in ourselves and others. With this awareness, we will be able to navigate situations and relationships accordingly.

In order to gather lessons from our lives, we need to take a step back and observe the bigger picture of our current situation. How are we attracting this situation? How is it connected to our personal history, especially our childhood? Patience is the key to unlocking the powerful wisdom our experiences bring to our awareness. As we sit back and slowly learn to read our behavioral patterns, the beauty, power, and value of our challenges and shortcomings will be unveiled.

Patience has been the hardest principle to integrate into my life. I learned the power of patience through my car accident, a head-on collision which fractured my sternum and injured my right knee. I had been driving along a country road one early morning, in a rush to hit the surf, when suddenly a car appeared in my lane, heading straight at me. I pushed the brakes and turned the wheel to get out of the way; but in a split second, I realized that I was going to hit the other car.

After the accident, I found myself unable to do anything. I couldn't walk without crutches. I couldn't get out of bed without help. I couldn't work. I couldn't surf. I couldn't participate in Ayahuasca ceremonies, which had become an integral part of my life. I couldn't even laugh without experiencing strong pain. For the first two months after the accident, I was only able to sit by the vegetable garden that I had planted. I prayed. I gave thanks for being alive and started a long process of healing that demanded my patience. Slowly, I accepted my situation. My mind wanted to go straight back to operating the way I did pre-accident, but my body moved at a much slower pace.

During this slow and arduous recovery, I came across the Native American art of crafting feather fans. The fans are extremely intricate, and greatly detailed in leather and bead-work. Fascinated, I began learning how to craft them. The key element was patience and a surrender to being in the present moment. The beadwork demands complete attention without distractions. Bead by bead, I started to see how beautiful patterns came alive on the handles of the fans. Beadwork created a channel for me to express myself in a new way, and it also showed me that, with patience, I could overcome the obstacles in my path to recovery. After three and a half months of little physical activity, I slowly started rehabilitation exercises. Just as I experienced the power of patience in my beadwork, I knew that my body would heal by focusing on the present moment and practicing patience. It took nine months to regain the strength to surf again, and almost a year and a half to return to the level of fitness and surfing that I had before the accident.

The beauty of accidents and ailments is that there is only one way out. Moving through the pain and discomfort and coming out on the other side gifted me with extremely valuable lessons. Even though I had my fair share of days when I was frustrated, depressed, and uninspired, finding valuable lessons helped me move through the difficulties. Every time I learned something, I made progress on my recovery path.

The Universal Energy always has a way to test our progress and cement its lessons in us. After the accident, I thought I had learned what it meant to be patient. But two years later, I contracted malaria. Then, over the next few years, I suffered from several smaller injuries. Throughout my recoveries from these injuries and ailments, I was able to maintain a positive attitude and keen awareness of which lessons were ready to harvest. Most recently, the patience I've cultivated by enduring these experiences helped me maintain my center and sense of peace during the coronavirus pandemic.

Exercise

One of the easiest ways to cultivate patience is by learning a new handicraft. No matter our age, learning something new involves a slow and steady progress towards mastery. The lessons of our craft-learning process will mirror the lessons of our inner development process. As adults, we have grown accustomed to performing tasks with precision, speed, and quality. Tackling something completely new helps develop patience. Take a moment to contemplate which elaborate craft resonates with you. Painting, pottery, knitting, model building, stained glass, beading, etc., are all good examples. Give yourself ample time to develop the craft without pressuring yourself. Commit to making at least three objects in whichever craft you choose.

THE EIGHTH PRINCIPLE: FORGIVENESS

 "The weak can never forgive. Forgiveness is the attribute of the strong."

—Mahatma Gandhi

We will never feel complete unless we forgive ourselves for the mistakes, pain, and suffering we have created for ourselves and others. We can live with honesty, integrity, commitment, compassion, courage, respect and patience; but if we cannot let go of rage and anger, we will be stuck in resentment with ourselves and others, until we learn how to forgive and let go. Without forgiveness, we will also never understand the value of our own mistakes and the crucial role they play in our healing and growth. Forgiveness brings acceptance and opens the door for healing the most uncomfortable and vulnerable inner wounds, conditioning, or trauma. It also allows us to grow in gratitude, once we have gathered the lessons from our healing processes.

Forgiveness is particularly important when we make mistakes, and perhaps even repeat them. If we are making the same mistake repeatedly, we should not beat ourselves up over it. We have simply not yet recognized the lesson of the situation at hand. If we judge ourselves, or fail to take responsibility for contributing to that situation, or take a victimhood stance, we create more work, making it harder to learn our lessons and move forward. We need to forgive ourselves for failing to see the situation clearly and change our perspective, realizing that something we need to learn is being brought to the surface, so we can address it. Once we can see this, we will be able to navigate the recurring pattern in a new way. The Universal Energy constantly tests us to ensure that we practice what we are learning. The beauty of our mistakes, wounds, traumas, or conditioning is we can learn from them, if we are open to it.

When we forgive ourselves, we open the space for a deeper relationship with all our inner aspects. We must accept and embrace the good and the bad, the positive and the negative, our strengths and weaknesses. Embracing our wounds brings us unity. When we have not integrated all aspects of our inner selves, we feel as if we are being pulled in different directions. This may be draining, making it difficult to move forward in our self-development path. For example, we may crave intimacy, but because we have been wounded from past relationships, we don't allow ourselves to commit or be loved. Or we might desire a trusting friendship with someone we've recently met, but resist it and maintain distance because of a past experience in which we were manipulated and hurt by a friend. In these cases, our wounds push in one direction and our longings in another. As we heal, learn, and grow from our experiences, we start the process of bringing unity to our entire internal world. This unity allows our mind, body, emotions and soul to work together, instead of against each other. As we bring peace to our inner turmoil, we have more vitality available to heal, learn, and grow. Without forgiveness, we will never experience lasting healing and growth. Forgiveness allows us a second, third, or fourth chance to learn from our mistakes. It brings peace to our troubled past, as it opens our Heart-Center to the deepest aspects of true love.

As I have mentioned, the relationship with my mom has posed some of the biggest challenges to my spiritual development process. For a long time, I held a grudge towards her for everything that had happened between us. This anger was hindering my ability to heal, and I was frustrated by it. A friend suggested I try family constellation therapy, which aims to heal generational traumas. While engaging in this therapeutic session, I learned about the dynamics between my mother and her own mother, and how those dynamics had shaped my relationship with my mom. Understanding the conditioning my mom had been exposed to while growing up diffused my anger tremendously. I could not be angry at her anymore and was eventually able to forgive her. I understood that I needed to create a new relationship with her, because I had been relating from a wounded space. I did a series of separation visualization exercises (see Appendix) to cut the energy cords with her so I could establish a new relationship from Heart-Center to Heart-Center. I never talked with her about it, but all the work I did allowed us to start relating in a healthier way. Forgiving her also freed up vitality I was previously expending on being angry. Forgiving myself for taking so long to forgive my mom was also a necessary step in this healing process.

Exercise

Find a comfortable place to sit and contemplate. Allow yourself to travel back through your memories, until you reach the first time you got in trouble with your parents as a little kid. Remember how you and your parents felt and their reaction to you. Now, forgive your younger self. Take a moment to sense how it feels to forgive and to be forgiven. Offer your younger self the explanation, compassion, and understanding you wish your parents had extended to you. Once you feel a completion of this process, move on to the next time you remember getting in trouble. Take your time moving through each memory. I recommend working through two or three memories each week, for as long as it takes to revisit incidents in which you feel the need to offer forgiveness to your younger self. At this pace, you will be practicing giving and receiving forgiveness on a weekly basis. Continue this practice for three to six months, to ensure that you have properly integrated forgiveness into your daily life.

CONNECTING THE DOTS

THESE PRINCIPLES CONSTITUTE a rock-solid foundation for our spiritual development, a source of strength in challenging times. The act of cultivating them permeates all aspects of our lives, enriching not only our personal practices, but also our relationships, work ethic, and contribution towards humanity as a whole. These Principles are the strongest spiritual foundation we can have as conscious humans. Thich Nhat Hanh compares consciousness to a fertile soil where all seeds can grow. As we cultivate the Universal Principles in our consciousness with our attention and dedication, they will grow into massive trees to dominate the landscape of our inner garden. When this happens, we reach a place within where we can experience true unconditional love.

Love is the brightest star shining in the night sky. This is not romantic love, but rather a greater love that encompasses all of creation. In order for universal love to flourish within, conditions must be right. We all have the potential to awaken the deeper aspects of universal love. These Principles constitute the eight pillars that sustain universal love. We can develop deep self-love only when we are living with commitment, integrity, honesty, respect, compassion, courage, patience and forgiveness. As we become aware of what it entails to live our lives based on these Principles and cultivate them within, we are able to apply them to every action we take, from touching our loved ones to making a business deal. Through embodying and practicing these Principles, true self-love flourishes and blossoms. From this inner space, we can relate to our environment and the people around us in a real and caring way. Caring for the state of the earth and its myriad inhabitants is a natural, and beautiful, side effect of reaching the inner space of deep self-love.

I envision humanity developing into its highest expression. We all have the capacity and the potential to find deep self-love within. That's the journey we owe ourselves to take on this lifetime, regardless of our profession, nationality, religion, race, or cultural heritage. We need to focus on our personal inner work as individuals. If we do, we can make the huge shift our planet deeply needs. As more of us commit to fostering our spiritual development, humanity will come closer to living in harmony with itself, and in balance with our Mother Earth.

CHAPTER II

ENERGY DYNAMICS

"If you want to understand the universe, we need to think in terms of energy and frequency."

— Nikola Tesla

ENERGY DYNAMICS FOR SPIRITUAL DEVELOPMENT

FROM A SPIRITUAL PERSPECTIVE, energy is a non-physical force or essence that binds the universe together. Everything in the universe is connected through energy and arranged by its frequency. Our actions, thoughts and emotions have specific energy frequencies. Every person, animal, plant, landscape, and place on the planet has an inherent energy frequency that determines how it's energy flows. Energies resonating at the same frequency attract each other, while energies resonating at different frequencies repel each other. Through understanding this concept, we start to grasp the inner workings of the Universal Energy. Since like-energies attract each other, we bring into our experiences what we carry within. Our actions, thoughts, and emotions actively broadcast a signal of energy, vibrating at a certain frequency, into the Universal Energy. The Universal Energy acts as a mirror, reciprocating our vibration with energies that resonate in the same frequency. Therefore, consciously or unconsciously, we are actively attracting the energies that match our inner state.

For example, when I was younger and living with my parents and siblings, I noticed how my sister developed a great fear of moths. We lived on the ninth floor of an apartment building in the city. Somehow, moths still managed to get into her room through the window. It happened repeatedly and in different locations. My room was next to hers, but moths never flew in through my window, which was always open, while her window was always closed. I recently asked her about this and she can't say exactly why she is so afraid of moths. Incredibly, after 25 years, she is still attracting them into her physical space, because she has not dealt with her fear of them. It's amazing how the energy dynamics work.

Our energy is composed of our thoughts, emotions, actions, beliefs, memories, wounds, traumas, and conditioning. Thoughts alone can create attraction, but under the influence of strong emotions, the attraction is amplified. For my sister, the strong fear of moths, and her actions that reinforced that fear, created a dynamo of attraction still spinning today. Repetitive thoughts, combined with strong emotions, broadcast a strong magnetic signal.

The mind is an extremely powerful tool and must be monitored to ensure it is broadcasting the proper signal. When centered, balanced, and under the right guidance, the mind can help us bring about love, joy, happiness, abundance, and prosperity.

Unchecked, the mind can create havoc in our lives, bringing about fear, misery, and sadness. The true leader within is the Heart-Center; the mind is only a tool. Our Heart-Center is our direct connection to creation and the source of our intuition. Through the Heart-Center, we have access to guidance from the Universal Energy—you can replace "Universal Energy" with God, Allah, Creator, Buddha, or the name of your highest divinity—that helps us through our development on Earth. The Heart-Center goes beyond reason, connecting with the Universal Energy that permeates creation at a level beyond the grasp of our minds.

The mind encompasses the conscious and the subconscious. While we are more acquainted with what is happening in our conscious mind, deep inner work requires digging into the subconscious, where the unhealthy conditioning we have acquired is stored. Accessing it can be a challenge. Being attentive to our reactions (which leaves no time for the conscious mind to be engaged) allows us to see what kind of patterns we are carrying. The process of inner work is three-fold. First, we need to acknowledge any subconscious conditioning influencing the situations in which we find ourselves. Then we must heal any emotional wounds left by those situations. Finally, we must figure out ways to care for ourselves, so we don't keep experiencing similar situations.

Our wounds, conditioning, and traumas cloud the connection to our Heart-Center. In our society, children are not generally encouraged to listen to their Heart-Center. However, we can reconnect with it, during the process of spiritual development, to restore the natural order of our inner world. We can accomplish this by healing our wounds, conditioning, and traumas, which allow us to reclaim our lives from the mind and return it to our Heart-Center.

As we proceed on this healing journey, it is important to develop clear boundaries around the attitudes and behaviors we will not allow into our physical, mental, and emotional space. Each time we allow in attitudes and behaviors that do not resonate with us, we send a message to the Universal Energy, telling it that we accept such attitudes and behaviors; and then more of the same is given to us. Before choosing which attitudes and behaviors we allow into our lives, we check in with ourselves; to determine whether or not the decision we are making is in alignment with our principles and spiritual development path.

We must also be vigilant about what is happening around us every day. Since all of creation is connected through energy, anything and anyone could be the carrier of messages or signs. If we pay close attention to our external experience and, at the same time, are aware of our internal process, we will be able to connect external occurrences with internal processes. In reality, "coincidences" are proof of the energy match that brings an event into our experience. For example, we may run into a person who shares something we needed to hear. Or we might keep encountering the same phrase in different sources. Or we repeatedly see a particular animal with which we have a connection. These are just a few examples that I have experienced when I needed to hear a message pertinent to my inner work process. Thus, we must be present in every step we take, so we can absorb the lessons we are attracting.

As we work on healing our wounds, traumas, and conditioning, we start to change our frequency. At first, we bring the wound, conditioning, or trauma to the surface of our consciousness, in order to work on it. This causes its energy to be present in our mental and emotional space; thus, we will attract similar energies into our lives. For this reason, we must be discerning with our social interactions, and the places we visit, during this healing process. Eventually, as we start healing the wound by acknowledging what happened, and forgiving ourselves or others, we are able to release the emotional load we've been carrying. When we do, we stop attracting the negative attitudes and behaviors associated with these experiences.

The exciting part is throughout this healing process, we learn many lessons. This allows us to connect lessons from different wounds as we discover their common thread. Eventually, we will be able to see a single clear and powerful lesson. As we encounter more situations where we can apply these lessons, we start embodying them, transforming the lessons into wisdom. Only by integrating the lessons, and acting accordingly, will our awareness shift, and will we no longer attract negative behaviors or attitudes into our physical, mental or emotional space. Depending on the severity of the wound, and how much it has affected us, we may need to approach healing it from different angles. This may require going through various processes, and even repeating cycles of healing. Therefore, it is so crucial to be committed, honest, and patient with our development.

. . .

Once we free ourselves from attracting and holding onto negative attitudes and behaviors, we start to experience a healthy momentum in our lives, and things start to fall into place perfectly and effortlessly. Ultimately, our true calling, or life purpose, will be revealed in this free and healthy inner space.

OUR INTERNAL ENERGY CENTERS

———

ACCORDING TO EASTERN SPIRITUAL PHILOSOPHY, the human body has seven main energy centers, located along the spine, through which energy travels. These energy centers are called chakras. Each chakra is associated with specific energies, colors, qualities, body regions, and organs. When these chakras are balanced, energy easily flows through them, and the body is healthy and centered. An imbalance in the flow of energy, due to a chakra being closed, or too open, affects the whole body system and the health of a person. Certain wounds, conditioning, or traumas may affect certain chakras and cause energy blockages between them. As we become aware of the qualities of each chakra, we gain perspective on the aspects of our inner selves that relate to each chakra and its importance to our spiritual development.

. . .

The first chakra, or root chakra, is located in the sacrum area. Its color is red, and its element is earth. It is associated with the physical body and with the adrenal glands, colon, kidneys, legs, and bones. It represents our survival instincts, self-image, security, basic needs (food, water, shelter), our physicality, sense of grounding, and our connection with ourselves. When this chakra is imbalanced, you might feel as if you are constantly living in survival mode. You may feel insecurity, dishonesty, defensiveness, greed, excessive negativity, anxiety, depression, or paranoia; and you might be inclined towards obsessive behaviors. All these symptoms are common in people with wounds, conditioning, or trauma affecting the root chakra. When the first chakra is well balanced, we develop confidence in decision-making and connecting with ourselves and others. We know of our value and are able to discern priorities, set goals, and fulfill them.

The second chakra, or sacral chakra, is located in the lower abdomen area. Its color is orange, and its element is water. It is associated with the ovaries, testicles, prostate, genitals, womb, and bladder. It is in charge of managing our sexuality, reproductive capacity, emotions, creative expression, passion, intimacy, and relationships. Second chakra imbalances are expressed as emotional problems and co-dependency with people or substances. Other indicators of an imbalanced sacral chakra may include lack of sex drive, obsessions about sex, manipulative behavior, emotional instability, lack of passion, self-doubt, or addiction. When the second chakra is balanced, we can express our sexuality in a healthy and balanced way. We are connected with our feelings and emotions and can express them. Our creativity is open, and we are using it. We are passionate in our beliefs. We are emotionally stable.

. . .

The third chakra, or solar plexus chakra, is located in the abdominal region. Its color is yellow, and its element is fire. It is associated with the digestive system, pancreas, adrenals, liver, gallbladder, and nervous system. It is in charge of processing food and transforming it into energy, personal power, autonomy, self-purpose, self-confidence, and self-esteem. Digestive problems, lack of self-confidence, or self-esteem, victimhood mentality, lack of motivation, workaholic habits, anger, lack of humor, subservience to others, shyness, and avoiding leadership are all symptoms of third chakra imbalances. When the third chakra is balanced, you feel self-confident and motivated. You have a sense of purpose and use your personal power to master your emotions. You are in alignment with your spiritual path.

The fourth chakra, or heart chakra, is located at the center of the chest. Its color is bright green, and its element is air. It is associated with the heart and circulatory system, lungs, thymus gland, arms, hands, and lymphatic system. It is in charge of our immune system, moving fluids through our bodies and giving us the ability to express love and forgiveness. In this chakra, the material plane and the spiritual plane converge. Fourth chakra imbalances are expressed as immune system or heart problems, lack of self-love, or lack of love towards others, fear and rage, self-pity, possessiveness, jealousy, and fear of rejection. When the heart chakra is balanced, you are able to feel love for yourself and others. You have the ability to accept and forgive yourself and others. You are compassionate and empathetic.

. . .

The fifth chakra, or throat chakra, is located at the throat. Its color is light blue, and its element is sound. It is associated with the thyroid, parathyroid, throat, mouth, tongue, and larynx. It is in charge of regulating our temperature, growth, and metabolism. It also governs our expression and communication. Fifth chakra imbalances are expressed as laryngitis or sore throats, thyroid imbalances, hearing problems, bronchitis, asthma, excessive talking, dishonesty, arrogance, problems of communication, lack of empathy, self-righteousness, manipulative tendencies, fear of speaking, lack of confidence in expressing feelings, gossiping, and lack of integrity. When the throat chakra is balanced, you are able to express your perspective and creativity with ease and grace. You are reliable, kind, and gentle. Communication flows easily, and you are sensitive to the impact of your words.

The sixth chakra, or third eye chakra, is located in the forehead, between the eyebrows. Its color is indigo, and its element is light. It is associated with the pineal gland, nose, eyes, and head. It is in charge of regulating the cycles of sleep and waking. This chakra is the connection to our intuition. Sixth chakra imbalances are expressed as sinus and/or eye problems. You may also feel stuck in your daily routine or out of touch with reality. You may lack clarity and feel disconnected from spiritual experiences. You may exhibit egotistical, impatient, or authoritarian behavior. When the sixth chakra is balanced, you feel in tune with the physical and spiritual realms. You are able to trust and follow your intuition. You can see situations clearly, have access to clairvoyant or clairaudience messages, and can read signs or omens in your daily life. You have the ability to visualize outcomes of situations. You are more sensitive to the subtleties of the energies that surround you.

. . .

The seventh chakra, or crown chakra, is located at the top of the head. Its color is white, and its element is energy. It is associated with the pituitary gland, the brain, the central nervous system, and the hypothalamus. It is in charge of orchestrating the perfect flow of energy through all our bodily systems. Seventh chakra imbalances are expressed as disconnection from spiritual matters. You may feel caught up in your head, or close-minded, or disconnected from your body. When the seventh chakra is balanced, you feel connected to God, the Universal Energy, and spirit. You are aware of a higher consciousness and are able to gather wisdom from your experiences.

This brief introduction to the chakras demonstrates that there are specific areas within ourselves where certain energies reside. All wounds, traumas, and conditioning can affect at least one of these chakras. Awareness of the chakras and their qualities helps us connect to our wounds, traumas, or conditioning. When we know which chakra or chakras are imbalanced, we can take a more focused approach with our healing and center our attention on these imbalanced areas. We can use affirmations (see Appendix) to target both the imbalanced chakras and the wounds, which supports healing, strengthen and reprogram them. The seven chakras comprise the seven major topics of our spiritual development. The first three lower chakras represent our connection to matter. The upper three represent our connection to spirit. The fourth chakra, or heart chakra, represents the connection between matter and spirit. This is the Heart-Center where we find the deepest wisdom, guidance, and transformation, which is why it is so important to live a heart-centered life. Our Heart-Center is the literal center of our being and serves as the true compass that guides us throughout our lives.

The key to bringing about a healthy and centered fulfilling life is to find the perfect balance between spiritual and material needs. If we focus only on our spiritual connection, we neglect our body and its needs, resulting in a major imbalance in the lower chakras. If we focus only on our material connection, our spiritual connection will be neglected, unbalancing our upper chakras. Only when we care for both our spiritual and material needs can we achieve a balanced, rewarding, and fulfilling life.

THE HEALING PROCESS

To DO inner work we need to dive deep into each situation that has caused us pain and suffering. If we feel emotionally triggered by an idea, person or situation, it means that a wound, conditioning or trauma needs our attention, awareness, love, and healing. Therefore, it is crucial to understand and integrate the Universal Principles into our daily lives. These Principles help create a solid foundation from which we can explore our emotions, some of which may be reactive and irrational. If we have a strong inner foundation, we can consciously choose to use each painful situation as an opportunity for inner work. At least, we can create the physical space to feel and process our emotions, and identify areas of our inner selves that we must work on healing.

We need to bring the healing essence of forgiveness and compassion to our darkest, most vulnerable, and tender places, along with the powerful light of our awareness. Surprisingly, the way to transform our wounds is to embrace them. It is normal to want to forget about what happened, to push away the memories and sweep our feelings under the rug. As humans, we don't want pain and suffering. However, in the process of exploring our wounds, we will find that the only way to heal them is to allow ourselves to feel the emotions we carry. Once we have honored our emotions, we need to re-center and balance ourselves to gather the valuable lessons our experiences have brought to the surface.

Each person has a unique way to heal their wounds, even though the process is similar for everyone. We must bring to the surface of our consciousness the situation that originally caused the wound. That alone is a huge first step. With those memories come emotions. Next, it's crucial to have a safe space from which we can properly release the emotions related to the wound. This safe space is protected both emotionally and physically from all external influences. If possible, it's a space where we can be supported by someone we trust, who can provide centering and grounding energy. In order to release the emotions, we must feel them fully and completely. We need to honor our feelings and give them the appropriate attention and space, both mental and emotional, so they can fulfill their life purpose: to be felt. Some may take longer to go through this process, depending on how long we have been storing them inside ourselves. We do what we must to release them: cry, laugh, get angry, scream, etc. After feeling our emotions, we let a couple of days go by. Once we are feeling better and lighter, we re-focus on the original wounding event. By now, we should not get triggered by the memories, because we released their emotional load. We won't forget what happened originally; our goal is to unearth the event's valuable lessons. If we are still triggered by re-examining the event, we repeat the emotional release process until we are able to look at the memories calmly. (The emotional release process is explained in detail in Chapter III.)

The next step is to forgive yourself for what happened to you, and for whatever you did that might have contributed to it. Forgiveness is powerful and opens the door to seeing the event's deeper lessons. After that, ask yourself: What is the lesson from this wound? When you are able to see the lesson, you will experience the transformation of pain into wisdom.

Keep in mind that it will take time, drive, mental and emotional space to move through these steps. Dealing with powerful emotions can be like going out into a storm at sea. Give yourself time after each incursion into your past. Experiencing long unfelt emotions can drain your vitality and make you feel exhausted. It is advisable to feel good and strong before beginning. You will have to follow this process with each memory that triggers you. Remember, with patience, time, and a self-loving approach, anything is possible.

Each process of inner development consists of various phases. As we deal with the emotions and challenges we are facing, our vitality levels will fluctuate. It is completely normal to feel drained, sensitive, or unmotivated as you are working through your wounds, conditioning, or traumas. It can be hard work, and at times even discouraging.

. . .

It is part of the human experience to feel the complete palette of emotions. A beautiful painting needs darker tones to serve as accents, creating a beautiful contrast to the lighter areas. We learn through exploring the contrast between our inner strengths and weaknesses. This is why we need to have a strong commitment with ourselves. We will be tested. At times, we will feel drained and unmotivated, but we must keep moving forward. Do not despair. This is part of the process. Muscles get stronger as they are used more. The challenges and obstacles we must work through as part of our healing process will ultimately help us build the inner strength that will carry us through to the end of a healing cycle. It is quite important to give ourselves enough rest when we need it. We might not be able to feel at our best for periods of time. We must stay present and focus on our process to avoid getting distracted. Remember, our healing is one of the top priorities of our life.

The beauty of our wounds, conditioning, and traumas is that, as we heal them, they can reveal great wisdom. They carry the lessons which will help us move forward. In a forest, old trees that die become compost on the ground, which in turn feeds the living trees. Likewise, our wounded self starts to die as we work on our healing, but the precious lessons gathered from the healing process will feed our new selves and propel us into bloom.

As we uncover the hidden gems of wisdom in our inner selves, we start the incredible process of transforming pain and suffering into lessons. As we integrate these lessons into our lives, we begin making connections between situations with common underlying threads. This is the way we transform lessons into wisdom.

When we work on our spiritual development, we begin developing a deeper way of seeing reality. We will not suddenly begin to see through walls; rather, we become able to see, or tune into, others and determine the progress of their own self-development journeys. As we do this, it becomes easier to discern which situations are good for us, and which ones we need to avoid or remove ourselves from. Through inner work, we can learn to read between the lines in our interactions with people.

However, this enhanced ability to see and feel more deeply and intuitively is a double- edged sword. We see more, but we may also judge more. Compassion for others is important now, as it is maintaining clear boundaries, so as not to allow unhealthy attitudes or behaviors into our mental or emotional space. If someone is exhibiting a behavior that we do not want to accept, it is important to express the discomfort. The person will hear us, and learn to respect our boundaries, or they will be unable to see what they are doing. In this case, it is best to remove ourselves from the situation.

When people are not ready to do inner work, trying to make them acknowledge their own unhealthy behavior can be a waste of time. It's like walking upriver; the energy is flowing in the opposite direction. You will feel exhausted, and the person may resent you for trying to get them to recognize something they are not ready to see.

. . .

The best way to determine the quality of our friendships and intimate relationships is to maintain strong boundaries and monitor reactions when we set and enforce boundaries. People who take the time to hear and respect our boundaries are the ones to keep in our life. Those who don't respect our boundaries are not worth our time and attention. Our family is an exception. We will always be in some kind of relationship with our parents, siblings, and extended family. We need to learn how to navigate their attitudes and behaviors in a way that supports our growth. It is important to know that the more inner work we do, the more our frequency changes. At some point, the personal priority disparities in certain friendships, or other relationships, will become apparent, and those relationships may end. It's normal to let certain people go from our life as our priorities change. As we define what is allowed into our mental, physical and emotional space, and what is not allowed, the Universal Energy will reciprocate our choices.

Note that setting boundaries can spark emotional reactions from others. To properly navigate these situations, and to see clearly how to make things right, let the heat of your emotions die down before choosing to engage in a disagreement. When people are emotionally triggered, their wounds, traumas, or conditioning are being touched. If you interact at such a time, you will be interacting with their wounds, rather than with them as an individual. Most people are overly attached to their wounds, conditioning, and traumas, because they have never healed from them.

. . .

For example, one of my landlords in California was quite controlling in the way he handled our common areas. Whenever I transgressed (rules were developed as new situations arose), he would be triggered, sending me a harsh text message informing me of his disapproval. At first, I tried to talk to him immediately, with unsatisfactory results. Even though I was acknowledging his side of the story, he was unable to see mine. This happened multiple times before I started delaying engagement. My new approach was to reply to the text message, then wait until the next day to speak with him personally. I began getting better results from our communication; the landlord was more understanding and developed rules that took both our sides into consideration. The key was allowing him the time and physical space necessary for his emotions to dissipate. That way, I could communicate with him, rather than with his wounds.

HEALING AND INTERPERSONAL RELATIONSHIPS

WHILE WE INTEGRATE and embody the lessons gathered from our inner work, we begin re-examining our relationships with family members, friends and partners. As I've mentioned previously, we change internally as we do our inner work. When these changes take place, we will be attracted to certain kinds of people and repelled by others. It is plain physics. We will begin to recognize that some individuals with whom we have relationships do not share our commitment to spiritual development. Consequently, some of these relationships may deteriorate. While this may be difficult, it is normal to cultivate relationships that add momentum to our development and to end those that become detrimental to it.

Of course, we are bound to some relationships, and we will not walk away from them. Our families, for example, can be used as a gauge to measure our development. We all know that spending time with family can bring challenges. We can use the time we spend with them to evaluate our embodiment of the lessons we have gathered.

We can also use the Principles to examine our other relationships. Maintaining relationships that are not based on commitment, honesty, integrity, respect, compassion, patience and forgiveness may be hindering us. On the other hand, it is important to recognize relationships that are based on these Principles and contribute to our growth and development. Those relationships are essential to cultivate and pour our time and attention into.

Communication is crucial. With our real friends, we can share our process and receive honest feedback. Others may lack the understanding, compassion, or love to hear about our process; they may disrespect our boundaries or be unable to help us with supportive energy. These people drain our vitality and take up valuable mental, physical, and emotional space in our lives. If we determine that some friendships are detrimental to our growth, it is wise to start phasing out these relationships. When we say no to friends who are unsupportive of our inner development process, we create space to cultivate better, and healthier, friendships.

Letting go of friendships can be hard, but necessary. I made a good friend during my time in Humboldt County. My co-worker "Tony" and I shared plenty in terms of cultural background, first language, and affinity for the Indigenous ceremonies (he was from Mexico). Tony was also learning from Jose, the Ayahuasca facilitator who was my mentor. Our friendship was good, until I had my car accident. He helped me through the worst part. Unfortunately, as I started to have certain realizations about my life, and shared them with him, our friendship started to change. I told him the work we were doing was not in alignment with my inner guidance. I could sense that he felt judged, even though I was not judging him for growing weed. In the end, I was offered a job in the Peruvian Amazon, and knew I would not return to Northern California. Through my commitment to my priorities and my choices, we grew apart. I had the physical, mental, and emotional space to start new friendships with a healthier foundation.

INTIMATE RELATIONSHIPS

WE ALL DESIRE the beauty of companionship, intimacy, and physical touch. That desire is embedded into our biology for the survival of our species. We are wired to seek a partner and reproduce. But sometimes we are victims of our own biology, and we engage in intimate relationships that are unhealthy.

We inherit from our parents their dynamics as a couple, healthy or unhealthy. As we grow up, we start attracting partners or lovers who match the dynamic that our parents had. If your intimate relationship has a healthy dynamic, you are lucky, and likely had good parental models. If it's unhealthy, you will need to do some intensive inner work to stop perpetuating the negative patterns you may have inherited from your parents.

. . .

When we enter the arena of romance and intimate relations, we also attract partners and lovers who match the dynamic we had with our parents. For example, if you are a man, the dynamic you have with a woman may mirror the one you had with your mom. If you are a woman, the dynamic you have with a man could be similar to the one you had with your dad. Any wound, conditioning or trauma that our parents carry affects us deeply. It is programmed within us as the baseline for our behavior as men or women, and our behavior with partners and lovers. If our dad wasn't present, we may attract male friends or lovers who also lack the ability to be present in our life, a situation that will continue until the original wound is healed. If our mom was overpowering or manipulative, we attract female friends or lovers with those traits as well.

Our wounds and traumas are likely to surface when we are in an intimate partnership, as this type of relationship requires us to be open and vulnerable. Our inner work and spiritual development will be tested many times in romantic relationships, providing opportunities to determine how well we have integrated and embodied the lessons that we have gathered.

To attract the right partner into your life, focus on your inner work to release unhealthy programming, heal your wounds and traumas, and learn to love yourself deeply. If anyone offers you love that doesn't match your deep self-love, you will know that it is not worth your time or energy to engage with that person. As you cultivate the Universal Principles within yourself, you raise the vibration of your mental, emotional and physical energy, increasing the likelihood of finding a partner who matches that frequency. A healthy and developed partner won't appear until you raise the bar within yourself, healing any wounds that might be limiting your potential for intimacy. In the end, the Universal Energy will bring a partner beyond what you can imagine.

DISCERNMENT VS. JUDGMENT

As we continue to dive deeper into our healing process, it becomes increasingly important to discern the situations and environments that may, or may not, contribute to our spiritual development. Discernment is the ability to see what is in alignment with the path we are choosing to lead, and what is not. For example, I kindly decline invitations to social events where alcohol is used as a means to connect with people. I know from past experiences that putting myself in these environments is not healthy for me. I have the discernment to say no, because drinking alcohol is not in alignment with my path of personal inner work.

Discernment is different from judgment, which is a formed opinion. For example, in the past I made decisions by judging certain situations or people. I judged people who chose to attend a party where there was alcohol, concluding that they had nothing to offer me, and even that they were bad people, because they chose to get drunk. I learned, though, that my thoughts often arose from judgment.

Judging people or situations does not help us move forward. It actually holds us in a frequency that prevents further growth. Letting go of judgment takes work, focus, and dedication, because judgmental attitudes are prevalent in modern society, and therefore deeply rooted in the subconscious mind. The antidote for judgment is compassion; remember, everyone on Earth is learning, and there is a purpose for everything and everyone under the stars.

We are all at different stages of our spiritual development. Everyone has something of value to learn from the situations they encounter in life, and as we learn and grow, the power of our choices improves or deteriorates our quality of life. Only with discernment can we choose wisely, letting the Universal Energy know what we want in our lives through the choices we make.

FINDING OUR OWN RHYTHM

DEVELOPING a healthy rhythm we can sustain for the long run has great importance as we nurture our spiritual growth. Unlike cleaning a house, where we can speed the process with technology, doing inner work has a pace of its own. We need to respect it from the beginning. If we push forward without listening to our inner selves, we can actually slow down the process.

Allow the pace of your inner work to be set naturally. You don't want to burn out. Taking small steps, while remaining fully present in the "now," is more sustainable than trying to run through the process and getting injured along the way. If you work consistently, small changes made daily or weekly will begin to add up. Eventually, you will experience a solid shift in your life that is not only real, but sustainable.

. . .

Throughout life, we go through various stages and sequences of healing and growth. Each time we begin a new phase, we must demonstrate a strong commitment to it. Otherwise, we may find ourselves easily distracted, or discouraged, from moving forward with our development.

The beginning phase of each process also demands vigilant care and compassion. Just as new seedlings are delicate when they begin to sprout and reach out into new territory, so are we during a new phase of growth. But like the seedling, our strength and resilience increase over time. And the more we integrate the Principles into our processes, the more momentum we gain, which helps us overcome obstacles with greater ease.

Each part of our growth process must come to completion in order to seal within ourselves the healing, lessons, and transformation. Similarly, we need to integrate the lessons into our lives for the new growth we are experiencing to become a solid part of ourselves. Until that is accomplished, we will be tested heavily; because the Universal Energy will bring us situations that challenge us to put into practice what we are learning. The time necessary for each process to bear fruit is unique to each individual, just as each plant fruits in its own season. This is when patience and commitment are crucial. Once we get to the flowering season, we become aware of individual lessons. We just have to pay attention, to make sure we don't miss them.

As we pay attention to the lessons and integrate them into our lives, harvest season brings forth the fruits of our labor. Our wounds begin to heal, and through our actions, we are able to combine all the lessons into wisdom. We can express gratitude for all that we have learned from our suffering. Once we have gathered the lessons and wisdom of a process, we finish a cycle and start a new one. If we look at life as an ever-ascending spiral, we circle through cycles, but revisit each cycle after a couple of years from a higher perspective.

A powerful tree grows from a tiny seed, overcoming all sorts of challenges and obstacles. In order to grow this powerful tree of inner wisdom, we need to plant adequate seeds. We must water, nurture and pull the weeds around them, preserving the water, food, and vitality for the tree we want to grow. Then we must be patient, allowing the tree to mature and share its bounty with us. In the same way, we need to give our attention, priority, and work to healing our wounds, traumas and overcoming our conditioning. As we invest our vitality and work in cultivating the Universal Principles, we create more momentum in our healing process.

Aside from what I have already shared, my car accident served as one of the greatest learning periods of my life. With plenty of time for contemplation, I saw that I was pushing forward to get all my inner work "done," which is unrealistic. Through the many days of recovery, I started to recognize the part of myself that pushed to keep doing more, while failing to integrate the many lessons floating in my awareness that I had yet to completely absorb and apply. That is when I understood the importance of a slower pace, realizing that I needed to take time to deeply integrate each lesson before moving on to the next. This allowed me to apply the lessons through my actions.

Because I was physically disabled, I embodied the process of slowing down. This new pace allowed me to develop deep respect for elders and people with physical limitations. I was also able to perceive the subtleties of this slower pace: how working on small changes every day leads gradually to perceivable shifts in the long run. Even though the recovery from the accident was one of the most challenging times of my life, it provided me with the opportunity to integrate many lessons, gave me a stronger connection with my inner self, and allowed me to feel the importance of finding a healthy rhythm of inner work.

LEARNING TO TRUST IN OUR INTUITION AND PATH

———

TRUST IS a critical element to spiritual development and healing. We must learn to develop a deep trust in our intuition. We need to trust our ability to go through the transformational processes of doing inner work. We also need to trust in the process, knowing that we are supported by the Universal Energy. If we fail to follow our intuition, we block our connection to spirit and may fall victim to our subconscious conditioning, causing us to act like robots programmed to act a certain way. When we trust our intuition, we are open to receiving the guidance our souls and hearts deeply crave. As we do inner work and develop a deeper trust in our own intuition, that trust is reciprocated by the Universal Energy. People start trusting us more, and opportunities appear at our doorstep.

Our intuition is always there to guide us. But each person experiences it differently. Some call it a hunch, a gut feeling, or a pull on the heart. The way in which our intuition presents itself is not important. The main thing is to develop a relationship with it. Most of us were not taught how to follow our intuition. Therefore, we have little trust in it. It's important to remember that intuition goes beyond the mind. Often, intuitive messages come quickly, before the conscious mind can even grasp them. And when we try to find the logic within the message, we end up ignoring the guidance.

To trust your intuition, you need to use it. It is like a muscle; the more you use it, the stronger it gets. Start with small, unimportant things, like where to go for a walk, or what to have for dinner. As you develop a relationship with your intuition, you will become comfortable following the guidance that you receive. Focusing first on unimportant matters will prepare you for big decisions later, and you will be certain then of the choices you need to make.

Sometimes we are being guided to take certain actions, even if we can't see the outcome. If it comes from our intuition, we need to jump in and trust that getting out of our comfort zone will allow us to expand to our full potential. I have embarked on journeys, even when I didn't know how to make them happen. But I trusted my intuition and the guidance I was receiving; I was then taken care of by the Universal Energy and received major lessons in the process, encountering beauty beyond anything I could have imagined.

I learned to listen to and hone my intuition as I pursued my travels to Peru. I had been offered work there as a translator, which was exciting. But then I learned that I would need to go sooner than I was prepared to. I had enough money to buy the ticket, but not enough to travel. I contemplated the proposition and received the feeling that I needed to buy the ticket, anyway. I bought the ticket and quickly lined up some work, so I could have some spending money while in Peru. But then, just as quickly as I had lined up the work, it was cancelled. I didn't have enough money to go, after all. I called a friend and told her about my situation. She loaned me money, so I could have a little cushion once I got there. Then, when I got to Peru, I learned I could not actually start working for another three weeks. I was baffled but continued to trust that things were unfolding this way for a reason. In the end, I was able to live comfortably off the money I had borrowed, and eventually I got to work. During the extra free time I had, I connected with people from whom I learned necessary lessons. In the end, I earned enough money to repay the friend who had given me the original loan. But she didn't want the money back, saying she wanted to offer it in support of my path. This is how it works when we trust in the guidance we are receiving. We are supported by the Universal Energy.

The Universal Energy knows how to create the proper setting to help us learn and grow. Trusting in your intuition and in the Universal Energy is a journey that takes time and effort; through the tests that come to us on our paths, we become stronger in our trust. Learning to trust is similar to birds learning how to fly. We can exercise our trust a little bit at first, providing ourselves with a soft cushion to land on in the safety of our nest; but we need to open our wings and jump out of our comfort zone to learn how to fly.

REVELATIONS OF OUR SPEECH

THE WAY we express ourselves reveals conditioning we may need to reprogram. It is paramount to pay attention to the words we use in certain contexts in order to see patterns in our everyday expressions that demonstrate unhealthy conditioning. Once we become aware of these patterns, we can make a conscious effort at changing the way we use certain words.

For example, someone who says, "I will try to do my inner work," is indicating a lack of commitment and respect. They're not being honest with themselves. Saying they are going to "try," instead of saying they "will do" their inner work, conveys the message that if something more important shows up, they won't do it. This demonstrates a lack of integrity, making it clear that the person lacks the level of self-love necessary to make inner work a priority.

. . .

I invite you to experience the difference between two sentences. Close your eyes and say to yourself, "I am going to try my best to make my inner work a priority in my life." How does the sentence make you feel? Now, say to yourself, "I will do my best to make my inner work a priority in my life." How does this sentence make you feel? Can you feel the differences between both sentences? The uncertainty of the first statement creates doubt and can dampen momentum. The certainty of the second sentence can provide motivation and positivity.

Our speech reveals the inner workings of our mind. Paying attention to the words and expressions we use can help us start to see how our minds compartmentalize concepts and experiences. Developing this awareness helps us identify recurring words and expressions that are rooted in a specific conditioning that we are working on. Let's say our goal is to develop our inner power. Any time we hear ourselves utter, "I can't," we need to stop and examine the source of that sense of self-doubt, and acknowledge the conditioning that has perpetuated it. Then we can start to make appropriate changes. The best way to counteract mental conditioning is by reprogramming our mind consciously through the use of affirmations. We will explore this technique in the Appendix.

In the process of reprogramming our mind we must be committed, consistent, perseverant, and have a good dose of self-discipline, because we will be dealing with years of conditioning. The old pattern has an established momentum and occupies precious mental real estate. Therefore, we need to work against the flow of established patterns for a while, until we start to tip the flow in a healthy direction.

REFLECTIONS ON THE STATE OF OUR HOMES

Our homes are sanctuaries where we retreat from the world to rest, nourish and replenish ourselves. But if these sacred physical spaces are not clean and in order, we will not benefit from the potential nourishment and regeneration they can provide. According to the Chinese practice of Feng Shui, there is an art to arranging physical spaces so as to influence the flow of energy within them. You may want to research various Feng Shui principles and apply them as best as you can in your home. It is most important to have a home space with inviting, positive energy. A disordered home creates tension and distress because of all the extra work needed to accomplish tasks within it.

The state of our homes reflects our internal state. It is important to pay attention to our tendencies and behaviors around the upkeep of our homes. With the proper awareness, we will notice when we are not attending to essential tasks. Then we can begin to examine our inner selves with the same attention. Are we neglecting areas that need tending?

For example, if you have a tendency to let dirty laundry pile up, until you have absolutely no more clothes, you may wish to examine whether or not you are avoiding attending to certain feelings, as well. If you tend to start home projects, but don't finish them, you may be demonstrating a lack of completion with internal processes. If you pay someone else to clean, rather than regularly cleaning up after yourself, you may lack responsibility for your internal processes, or have a tendency to overstep boundaries. Some of the fun of inner work is making the connections between exterior and interior tendencies in our behaviors. Determine what your exterior tendencies represent for you.

We need to create a sanctuary, a place of refuge and safety, in our homes. It is important to take the time to arrange our furniture so it projects a welcoming feeling every time we enter our home. Keeping up with the duties related to the upkeep of our homes ensures a renewal of energy and helps with our inner work.

I am adamant about keeping my home organized and clean. However, life is in constant flux, and sometimes I slack here and there. This reflects my internal process. Once I see where I have slacked, I make it a top priority to restore order and cleanliness. I generally schedule a big cleanup and organizational day once a month, as close to the new moon as I can. This creates a fresh start on the new cycle. Then I work in small bits throughout the month to keep my home the way I like it.

I saw how important the home space is for my inner work during my time in Hawaii. I lived there for five years, moving several times during the initial nine months there, until settling into the house where I lived for four years. My first year and a half in the house were excellent. Professionally, I had a success-ful, growing practice. Personally, I had a steady and healthy pace of growth in my inner work. My home was spotless and cared for. After my ex-partner moved in with me, my priorities and long-term goals started to change. I started to see the limita-tions I had surrounding my work, and how unfeasible it was to expand and grow it. The house we were living was not appro-priate for more growth. Recognizing these realities was a year-long process that allowed me to realize we needed to seek new horizons, where we could develop our professional projects. We reached the decision to move out of the US just as the pandemic started; therefore, we decided to wait a while before moving. Having made the decision to leave our home, however, I slacked in the cleaning and yard maintenance, which reflected my inability to make the changes we deeply and urgently needed. It wasn't until we bought tickets to leave Hawaii that my feelings of frustration started to lift and my care for my home space got back on track.

ADDICTIONS

As we work on our spiritual development, it is important to examine any addictions we may have. An addiction to a substance, behavior, or activity indicates deep, unresolved inner wounds. The addiction is a self-medicating mechanism to pacify pain and suffering, likely generated from a past wound or trauma. Not being able to go a day without a particular fix could indicate a major internal imbalance, and steps must be taken to reach the root of the addiction. The only way to heal it is by addressing the trauma or wound that's creating the pain and suffering.

Addictive patterns can be associated with illicit substances, sex, food, adrenaline sports, pornography, etc. It is important to understand that each person with an addiction is on a unique path. No one will be able to quit until they are truly ready. There are precious lessons to gather during the process of releasing an addiction from your physical, mental, emotional, and psychic space.

Addiction starts with the habitual use of a substance or behavior; eventually, the person relies completely on it to "get ahold" of their center, replacing life responsibilities with addiction. If you have a particular fix that you can't let go of, ask yourself why you are relying on coffee, donuts, drinks, or cigarettes. Through reflection, you'll eventually discover the root cause of the addiction. Understanding the energy behind the addictive behaviors reveals the way to heal them. (This reflective process works with mild addictions. People with more serious addictions need professional support to heal the originating trauma.)

Anything we put into our bodies that is detrimental to our health is self-abuse; this happens because we lack deep self-love. At times like these, we should ask ourselves what is making us uncomfortable. Usually, we are not listening to our internal guidance. In order to overcome addiction, we must listen deeply to our intuition and work on healing our wounds or traumas. When we free ourselves from these addictions, we reclaim our inner space from unhealthy behaviors, spark great momentum in our development, and gather priceless lessons. The best way to overcome an addiction is by replacing it with a constructive habit. As we begin working on healing our wounds, we start incorporating techniques that create healthy habits in our lives. By developing positive routines, we eliminate the empty inner space where addictions had been able to enter. (We will explore specific personal practices to aid in this process in Chapter III.)

. . .

I was addicted to cigarettes for ten years. Part of the addiction came from family conditioning. As a young boy I saw my mom, uncle, aunts, and great-uncle smoking, and I wanted to be like them. Part of the addiction came from wounds originating in my relationship with my mom. I tried many times to give up smoking, without success. I was able to be clean for a while, but then I'd encounter a situation that triggered the pain associated with my wounds and fall back into smocking. Then, during one of my isolation incursions in the Amazon, I saw how I was using the habit as a pacifying behavior; it allowed me to avoid feeling the pain of the original wound and trauma associated with my mother. It took forgiving myself and my mom for what had occurred between us to create the conditions that allowed me to let go of smoking. I started to develop a deeper self-love, which in turn created more care for my body. Once I recognized the root of my addiction and resolved to stop it, I was able to quit. It has been eight years since I quit it.

NATURAL RHYTHMS

EVERYTHING in the natural world is dictated by a particular rhythm that ensures and maintains the balance of life. The revolution of the Earth around the sun creates the seasons, each of which has a peak moment of change marking the shift into a new season. These are the solstices and equinoxes. There are also periodic moon cycles, which have profound effects on Earth. It is beneficial to pay close attention to these events throughout the year. Since we are connected to the larger cosmos, the seasonal changes that affect the Earth affect us, as well. Indigenous peoples around the world are in tune with these changes, and many of them have rituals, celebrations, or ceremonies at the peak moments of these natural cycles.

Solstices mark the end of the old cycle and the beginning of the new one. The Summer Solstice marks the longest day of the year and the period when days begin to shorten. It is a time to honor the light, a time to look outward and be open to action. The Winter Solstice marks the shortest day of the year, when days begin to lengthen. It is a time to honor the darkness, to look within and slow our pace. The equinoxes represent the midpoints between solstices, when the length of the day equals the length of the night. This is a time to honor the balance within ourselves.

We also need to be aware of lunar and solar eclipses. They provide windows into the beginning of a particular cycle of our spiritual development. There are, on average, two solar eclipses and four lunar eclipses per year. Each eclipse cycle lasts roughly six months. Different areas of our lives may be impacted by these eclipses, depending on when they occur, and what astrological sign is associated with that time of year. For this reason, we must familiarize ourselves with astrology—not the type in a newspaper column—that tells us how to make money or find love. The astrology I am talking about lets us know which areas of our lives will be under celestial influence at certain points in time, depending on where planetary events are happening.

Distant stars form constellations that act as a background for our immediate solar system. Each constellation represents a particular set of aspects of our lives, with specific qualities that affect us physically, emotionally, and mentally here on Earth. Understanding where in the constellations a planetary event will occur enables astrologers to know what kinds of tendencies will be more prevalent during certain events, or which areas of our lives will be most impacted. These planetary events include solstices, equinoxes, solar and lunar eclipses, new moons and full moons; but there is more to explore when we take into consideration all of the planets in our solar system. All these events mark peak moments of energy that bring forth particular aspects of our inner work.

Keep in mind that I am not asking you to become an astrologer. I am simply encouraging you to be aware of the cycles and tendencies at play all around us. In pre-industrial society, following the rhythms of nature closely was part of everyday life. We have since disconnected ourselves from these natural rhythms. Consequently, we have become unbalanced and uncentered. By following and being aware of the major plane-tary cycles, we start to develop an innate relationship with the natural flow of life. Astrology provides us with extra awareness, showing us which areas of our lives are influenced at different points throughout the year. I encourage you to research for yourself and learn more about the exalted times of the natural cycles: solstices, equinoxes, eclipses, and the lunar cycles.

LUNAR CYCLES

THE MOON IS the only natural satellite of the Earth and has a powerful influence over our lives and the environment. The moon rules the waters of the Earth. The tides of the ocean fluctuate in rhythm with the cycles of the moon. Peak tides happen under new and full moons. Spiritually speaking, water represents our emotions, and the moon's effect upon us emotionally is tangible, once we start paying attention to its cycles. When we begin to pay attention to these cycles, we may notice that people are more emotional, and there is a higher level of intensity at play, on days closest to the new moon or full moon.

Each new moon, we start a new cycle, with a particular theme for the month, depending on the constellation in which the moon is situated. For example, if the new moon falls in the sign of Scorpio, the month's themes revolve around going deep with ourselves, transformation, and healing. If the new moon falls in

Sagittarius, the themes of the month revolve around adventure, traveling, expansion, and optimism. The full moon acts as a magnet, bringing to the surface emotions that have not been dealt with, so we can acknowledge and release them. Awareness of the new moon and full moon astrological signs enables us to work with the lunar cycles to focus on different areas of our inner work. With its renewing tendencies, the new moon helps us start processes by closing the previous cycle and starting a new one. The full moon helps us to feel and release our emotions.

Information provided by astrologers helps me set my intentions for each lunar cycle, aiding me to focus my attention on areas of myself related to the theme of the month, eclipse, solstice, or equinox. As we work with the cosmic cycles, we have reference points to use as landmarks for all the work we have done. It is crucial to become in tune with moon cycles as a way to get back in touch with natural cycles in general.

MERCURY RETROGRADE

OF ALL THE planets in our solar system, Mercury occupies a special place, because it brings constant fluctuations in tendencies to our spiritual development processes. In astrology, Mercury is considered the messenger, associated with all forms of communication. It also influences technology, scheduling, and transportation.

Mercury is the closest planet to the sun, taking only 88 days to orbit around it, compared to the Earth's 365 days. The time difference in the orbits of Mercury and Earth create an astrological phenomenon called retrograde. It happens 3-4 times a year for a duration of 3-4 weeks. During a retrograde, Mercury appears from Earth to be going backwards in its orbit. This is an optical illusion created by the movement of Earth as we look at Mercury. All other planets in the solar system go through a retrograde as well, but not as frequently; and their influence is

FROM WOUND TO WISDOM

not as pronounced as Mercury's retrograde. Since our society relies heavily on communication technology, the retrograde effects of Mercury are more tangible than retrogrades of other planets.

Mercury's retrograde is a time best used to slow down and take a look back at the last several months of our lives. What parts of ourselves have we been working on? In what areas did we experience improvement? What areas are we having difficulties with? The prevalent tendencies of Mercury's retrograde are conducive to deep inner work, self-exploration, healing, and transformation—hence, the need to slow down and listen. During Mercury's retrograde, it is normal to experience miscommunications, delays in paperwork, phone and computer mishaps, and other technological glitches. You may also experience miscommunications in face-to-face conversations.

You don't have to put your life on hold during a Mercury retrograde, but it is helpful to be aware when we are going through it. The prevalent tendencies of the retrograde will prompt the need to backtrack to mend any mistakes or misunderstandings. If you know you are in retrograde season, you can be more conscious in the way you express yourself to avoid miscommunications. You can double-check important correspondence, to make sure it arrived. You can also spend more time by yourself to absorb the lessons from your spiritual development process.

The retrograde season highlights an important part of our development process. We cannot be pushing forward all the time. We need to tune in to the ebb and flow of the Universe in order to feel the prevalent tendencies of each moment. When it is time to sow our seeds, we do so. When is time to harvest the fruits of our labor, we do so. If we are trying to plant in harvest season, we are going against the energy flow. Therefore, it is important to be aware of Mercury's retrograde. It is a periodic reminder from the Universe to check in with ourselves.

CONNECTING THE DOTS

WE ARE NOW aware of the dynamics of our choices, priorities, wounds, traumas, and conditioning. We also understand how we are affected by the monthly cycles of the moon, as well as the planets as they orbit the sun.

As we dive into our past, we bring our wounds, conditioning, and traumas to the surface of our consciousness to heal, learn, transform and grow. Our personal cycles are in connection with the cosmic cycles, including lunar motions, solstices, equinoxes, eclipses, and other planetary alignments. Such cosmic events can be seen as cornerstones that mark the beginning, or end, of a particular cycle. This allows us to take advantage of the prevalent tendencies of a particular cosmic event, using it to further our development and increase our growth momentum. As we can see, we are always in a cycle within a cycle within a cycle, illustrating the fractal quality of the Universe and highlighting the never-ending learning that our souls need for expansion and growth.

When we first start addressing our wounds, conditioning, and traumas, we have a backlog of many years to address. That's why it's important to properly cultivate the Universal Principles within. With a solid inner foundation, we move through processes and cycles; and eventually, we catch up with the backlog. However, this is not the end of our inner work. We continue to live and have experiences. Some will be challenging; we will need to process, digest and gather lessons from them. Yet we now have practice and understand the processes, which allows us to move more gracefully through our growth. Learning and growing is a continual process, as long as we are alive. As we will see in the next chapter, our different practices give us a way to navigate our growth, anchoring lessons and wisdom deep within our being.

CHAPTER III

DEVELOPING YOUR PRACTICE

" Practice makes perfect. After a long time of practicing, our work will become natural, skillful, swift and steady."

— Bruce Lee

DEVELOPING A SOLID PRACTICE

WE NOW CARRY the deep awareness needed to move forward on our spiritual development path. But awareness alone won't change our life or heal our wounds. Forward momentum is created through conscious implementation of the Universal Principles, developing a daily practice, facing our deepest wounds, and accounting for energy dynamics in our choices and actions. It all comes down to what we do in the present moment.

It is crucial to cultivate a daily practice, by which I mean a personal set of activities to connect with our inner self, listen to our intuition, set intentions for the day, and maintain a healthy relationship between our mind, body, and spirit. This daily routine will become the backbone of our healing, transformation, and growth. However, daily practices alone won't heal wounds and traumas. We need to address each trauma and wound with a process I call "emotional release." This enables us to release the emotions attached to our memories. When we allow this process to happen, powerful lessons arise. Our daily practices will help us move through the emotional release process. We must also be aware that all aspects of ourselves are interconnected. The different parts of our practices will help support the healing process we initiate to address our wounds, conditioning and trauma.

Our most important priority in life is our own well-being. If we are not centered and balanced, we cannot move forward in our development or support others. Therefore, we need to develop enough self-love to allocate a certain amount of time each day for self-care. This can be difficult for some people; but creating a daily practice is healing and beneficial. The consistency builds momentum and connection; and it motivates us to keep reaching deeper every day. Since each individual is unique, personal practices vary greatly. The necessary common elements are mind maintenance, body maintenance, and spiritual maintenance. Neglecting any area creates an imbalance. Some practices can be done 2-4 times per week, some bi-weekly, some twice a month, some once a month, and some only when needed. Be aware that some practices can address several, or even all, of the areas we seek to maintain. For example, a hike through the woods is beneficial for the body, relaxes the mind, and reminds us of our spiritual connection to nature, which resonates in perfect balance with creation. If I feel out of balance, I immerse myself in nature to return to balance. Our intuition will guide us regarding the frequency of our practices.

· · ·

Mind maintenance encompasses all kinds of meditation, visualizations, affirmations, and breath work. It also includes reading about or studying topics to help us expand and grow. This practice helps balance the mind and addresses our conditioning.

Body maintenance encompasses aerobic and anaerobic exercises. Individually suitable cardio exercises, such as hiking, running, swimming, and cycling, are necessary to maintain a healthy body. Stretching exercises are important also, to maintain flexibility and help release muscle stress. (Yoga is a great practice for this.) Physical exercise maintains our vitality, keeps our stamina levels up, and helps us ground ourselves in our bodies.

Spiritual maintenance encompasses practices that feed our spiritual nature. These can be rituals, ceremonies, religious practices, or prayer, depending on each person's background, heritage, or religion. However, spiritual maintenance is not limited to these activities. Some people find spiritual sustenance in climbing mountains or surfing big waves; everyone's needs are different. That's why it is important to listen to and follow our intuition. It will unfailingly guide us toward growth and transformation.

MIND MAINTENANCE

OUR MINDS HAVE INCREDIBLE POWER. Our challenge is to harness and channel that power through an avenue we choose, rather than allowing our conditioning, wounds, and traumas to dictate where we spend that power and vitality.

We are aware of the duality of our minds. The conscious mind is easier to work with, because it is more visible, tangible and we have control over it. On the other hand, we have little control over the elusive subconscious mind, which is more subtle and reactive, and arises when we are triggered. For example, we may not possess enough self-love to provide our body with healthy foods; nevertheless, we can consciously make an effort to change our diet. But this won't automatically change the way we feel about ourselves. We may have an underlying conditioning or wound, resulting in a lack of self-love, that is expressed as an unhealthy eating habit. We need to heal the wound and consciously create programing to replace the unhealthy conditioning. If we do not, it will resurface.

This is where the daily practice reveals its power. As we go through cycles of the emotional release process, daily balancing exercises support our healing work. These exercises allow for clarity of vision, powerful self-affirmations to nurture and strengthen the wound we have brought to the surface, and breathing exercises to foster a strong connection between mind, body and spirit. Although I have listed meditation, affirmations, and breathing exercises under mind maintenance, these exercises also bring balance, healing, and growth to our body and soul.

BODY MAINTENANCE

OUR BODY IS the home of our mind and soul. Without our bodies, we are not human. In order to live a vibrant, balanced, and awakened life, it is extremely important to give the proper attention and care to our bodies. If we fail to provide this care, our health will suffer, decreasing our quality of life. With the vitality and resources we possess, we must consciously choose to eat healthy foods that nourish our bodies; develop wholesome habits that promote vigor; and exercise regularly to maintain a healthy, strong body.

Exercising and stretching regularly is highly beneficial, because it helps us to be in the present moment. It also contributes to being more connected to our bodies and the physical plane, allowing us a break from the mind. Through exercise, we detoxify our bodies by sweating. We also develop physical strength and attain a sense of well-being.

. . .

It is paramount to be honest with yourself and understand your current physical condition. If you're out of shape, start slowly, building the muscle capacity to perform longer and more demanding exercises. I have gotten injured multiple times, resulting in a decline of the physical condition I once had. Recovering from injuries is challenging; the mind wants the body to return to its original capacity, but the body can't recover so quickly. This is how I learned to listen to my body and work with its limitations. I started slowly, with a consistent and self-disciplined approach. Over the course of 6-8 weeks, I was able to get back to my pre-injury physical condition. Don't push too much or too soon. As when doing inner work, push yourself just outside your comfort zone. By slowly expanding your comfort zone, you can exercise more intensively as you honor yourself and grow. It is also important to have regular rest days, when you take a break from exercising or stretching, the body has the needed time to replenish its energy. Again, listen to your body and your intuition to find the perfect frequency and intensity of exercises.

Regular exercise and stretching help release mental and physical stress and tension as well as stagnation and lassitude. We need an active lifestyle to get into our "zone," the internal space we reach when we are in tune with ourselves. Here, we can better navigate with ease and grace the energies we encounter daily. As a result, we experience great joy, growth, and expansion.

SPIRITUAL MAINTENANCE

WE HUMANS ARE COMPLEX BEINGS. Just as we need
sustenance for our minds and bodies, we have an innate need to
feed our souls as well. Only when we are actively working to
balance the mind, body, and spirit are we able to gather the
guidance and wisdom that show us our path.

We lived originally in tribal societies, intimately connected to
the cycles of nature, which dictated daily life. As a result of
industrialization and capitalism, we modern humans have
become disconnected from nature. It is an important part of our
spiritual maintenance to use the natural cycles as a way of
getting back in synchrony with nature, which helps us get in
sync with all of creation. We do not need to restrict our regular
practices to the exalted times of natural cycles (new moon, full
moon, equinoxes, solstices and eclipses); but it is especially
important to remember to practice at those peak times.

. . .

Daily meditation, affirmations, or breathing exercises help calm and center the mind. They also help develop more connection with the soul. Additional practices that help us process our experiences include journaling, painting, music, weaving, beadwork, etc. These activities engage both sides of the brain, allowing us to dissipate the emotions from our inner work. They also help us drop into a contemplative space, so lessons can arise. I encourage you to find practices that work and resonate with you. The process of creating art brings healing, regardless of the results. So even if you are not a painter or a writer, the experience of painting or writing will benefit your inner work process.

We use the exalted times of the month to do deeper inner work, because the tendencies of new moon, full moon, equinox, solstice, or eclipse are more conducive to it. Keep in mind that the rest of society will be engaged in "normal" mode. Sometimes the celestial event occurs in the middle of the week, which makes it impractical to engage in deeper and more demanding processes. If this is the case, start by setting your intentions or saying some prayers for your process on the day the event is happening; then use the coming weekend to go through the ritual or ceremony.

As I shared earlier, the lunar cycles, solstices, equinoxes, and eclipses are powerful times of planetary alignments. Using these moments to connect with ourselves and engage in ritual, ceremony, or prayer, allows us to develop a deeper relationship with the cycles of nature; and we are using the prevalent plane-tary tendencies to fuel our momentum.

The purpose of the ritual, ceremony, or prayer is to create time for contemplation, processing, releasing, healing, transforma-tion, and growth. We can use the ritual to let go of old behav-iors, release emotions or traumas from past events, honor our feelings and experience, and honor the closing of one cycle and the opening of a new one (In the following section you will find instructions for an emotional release ritual).

Our mind, body, and spiritual maintenance practices constitute the outer structure of our inner work and allow us to process and integrate our experiences (Cultivation of the Universal Principles constitutes the inner structure of that work). Throughout our lives, we experience events that need proper processing and integration. However, those raised without an understanding of inner work must first address a backlog of trauma, wounding, or conditioning experiences. Moving forward with healing, growth, and transformation takes time, work, and application of the Universal Principles.

THE PROCESS OF INNER WORK

We now are aware of the connection between our lives and all the aspects of ourselves. We know we need the strong foundation of the Universal Principles to face our most vulnerable, wounded, and sensitive areas. We have also developed maintenance practices that help us move forward through the actual process of inner work. All these elements will help us move through the steps necessary to face old wounds, traumas, and conditioning that are negatively affecting our lives. This is what inner work is: bringing to the surface of our consciousness the parts of ourselves that need our attention, love, forgiveness, and healing.

The process of inner work is delicate. It demands effort and our full attention, and is not something we do every day. It is best to prepare to engage in this work at a time conducive to it, such as during the exalted times of the month or year. We must also have a proper physical space, where there will be no disturbances or interruptions.

Our intention is a powerful element of the inner work we do. A clear intention sets the tone for a practice or ritual. The questions below are meant to guide you into the areas of yourself where unresolved matters need attention, healing, and growth. These questions will help you develop intentions for the emotional release process. Take your time answering them. You can journal about each question that resonates with you, but do not be shy about asking additional questions of your own. Use these questions as examples, and allow yourself to be guided towards other questions you can ask yourself, to help you go deeper within. You can also write down your intentions after you answer the questions.

- Have you experienced any traumatic events in your life? If so, do you feel at peace with the event, and what did you learn from it?
- Do you feel you need help in any areas of your life?
- Are there any similarities between your current situation and the family dynamics you experienced during your childhood or teen years?
- Do any specific situations trigger you? If so, list the triggers.
- Is there any connection between your childhood or teenage family dynamics and your current triggers?
- Are there uncomfortable situations that keep recurring in your life? If so, ask yourself, "How am I attracting this situation into my experience?"

Having answered your questions, you now have a personal map of the areas you need to work on. Keep in mind that you will not address everything at once. You will address each event separately, going through the emotional release process described below. With each process, you will bring to the surface of your consciousness the energy - memories and emotions - from your wound or trauma. This energy will be present in your inner space while you heal. It is a process that varies from person to person and may take a couple of days, or last several weeks, depending on the severity of the trauma, the length of time since it occurred, and the pace at which the event can be healed and integrated.

Make sure not to put yourself in unhealthy places before, during, or after going through these processes. As you release past events and initiate healing, the energy you let go is present in your mental and emotional space; hence, you have the potential to attract more of such energy. A bar, therefore, is a dangerous place to go after doing deep inner work. It is also important to refrain from spending time with people who drain you, or are unable to respect your boundaries, during this process. You need all your vitality now. You can be more sensitive than normal after an emotional release process, you must give yourself the time and emotional space for healing to occur before entering situations where you must be strong or protect yourself.

THE EMOTIONAL RELEASE PROCESS

This is the way I like to set up the physical space for an emotional release process. Sit on the floor or a chair. Turn off any artificial lights, and light one or more candles. Set your intentions and go through the steps below.

. . .

Have someone present for support, if you feel you need it. This person needs to hold space for you, which means that they won't judge you and will be a grounding presence, helping you go through your process.

- Do a 15-minute grounding meditation to center yourself. (Appendix)

- Give yourself permission to revisit the incident you wish to process.

- While being present with your breathing, find the memory from the wound or trauma you wish to work on.

- Allow the memory to surface to your consciousness by focusing your attention on it and seeing it replay in your mind.

- Allow emotions attached to the memory to rise up, as well. The emotions must be felt, so they can fulfill their life cycles.

- Honor your emotions by feeling them without judgment. Pain, sadness, frustration, anger, grief, disgust, indignation, fear. It is completely normal for any of these emotions to surface around our wounds or traumas. If you need to cry, allow yourself to do so freely.

. . .

- Give yourself enough time for the feelings to subside. The first step towards healing from a wound or trauma is forgiving yourself for having to endure such an experience. Our souls choose the conditions we come into on Earth. On a deep level, we put ourselves in harm's way for our own spiritual development. Allowing the emotions you summoned to subside can take a while. If you feel drained at this point, you need to end the process. Express your intention of ending the process and do a 5- to-10 minute grounding meditation to ground and center yourself. Then give thanks for the process, blow out the candle, and do the body scrub and flower bath described below. Once you have the vitality to resume, you can pick up where you left off.

- If you feel you have the capacity to move forward, do the separation visualization associated with the person who hurt you (described in the Appendix).

- Do a 5- to 10-minute meditation to ground and center yourself. At this point, you can offer prayers for healing and growth. Give thanks to the fire (candle) for the process, and finish by blowing out the candle.

I want to express my support to you and your healing for having the courage to go through the emotional release process. It is not easy, which is why so many wounded people are walking around this planet, unable to heal their traumas. It takes courage to revisit a painful event, and it's normal to feel extra-sensitive, tired, and drained afterwards. It's important to rest the next day and replenish your vitality. During the few days to several weeks it takes for the emotions to settle completely, you will not experience them with the same intensity that you did during the release process; but the emotions will be present in your day-to-day life in some form. In the two weeks following the process, you can use journaling, painting, music, beading, and other kinds of crafting, combined with your mind and body maintenance practices, to help digest your experience. Take time to contemplate what happened. You may feel as if you've already learned key lessons from the experience; but don't stop yourself from looking deeper within for even more profound lessons. This becomes crucial once you have completed several healing processes, because you will begin to identify patterns and make connections. The more this happens, the deeper the lessons that will be revealed.

The purpose of this work is to match traumatic situations in our past with recurring problematic situations in our present, and with our triggers. Triggers are signposts pointing toward discomforting areas within ourselves that need attention and healing. Addressing these areas allows us to release their emotional charge and perceive the lessons they are ready to yield. As we do so, we begin to reprogram ourselves, letting go of conditioning that no longer serves us. It is paramount to put into practice what we learn from our past. If we don't apply the lessons, we are not integrating our emotional release process properly into our lives. As we begin to glean the lessons from these processes, our internal state starts shifting. However, only when we start applying the newly gathered lessons will our growth and healing seal properly.

ENERGY CLEARING PRACTICES

AFTER AN EMOTIONAL RELEASE PROCESS, a lot of emotional energy is emanating from our psychic spaces. The body scrub and flower bath described below is not mandatory, but it can help speed the discharge of those energies, which are related to the original trauma. Our intention, combined with the salts, lemon, essential oils and flowers helps release the emotions of the trauma, facilitating the healing process. It's best to use this technique right after an emotional release process. If you can't do it right away, make sure to do it the following morning.

Body scrub

This body scrub can be used any time you feel the need to clear your mental, emotional, or psychic space.

· · ·

Ingredients:

- 2 cups of Epsom salts
- The juice of 2 lemons
- 5-6 drops of tea tree essential oil
- 5-6 drops of lavender or frankincense essential oil

In a bowl, pour the 2 cups of Epsom salts, followed by the lemon juice and the drops of each essential oil.

Add one cup of water and mix. The consistency should be watery, but not so much that the salts dissolve completely.

Speak your intentions into the preparation. You can say them aloud or quietly. For example, you might say something like, "My intention is to release all the emotions associated with this specific trauma. I let go of the pain, suffering, and conditioning, allowing space within myself to open for learning, healing, and growth."

Gently scrub your entire body with the mixture while you are in the shower. You don't need to put it on your hair, though. If you feel the need to apply it to your head, just use some of the liquid. Be careful with your sensitive areas, because the mixture can be abrasive if you apply too much pressure. Make sure you scrub behind your ears, as far as you can on your back, and between your fingers and toes. Be thorough. Save some for the end, and pour it below your neck on your back, so your entire body is covered by the mixture. Once you have finished, take a warm shower to rinse the mixture from your body.

Flower Bath

The flower bath is another optional practice to support and boost the healing process. If it resonates with you, try it out. I learned this practice in the Amazon jungle, where it has been used to aid spiritual healing for longer than Western medicine has existed. Granted, most of us don't have access to the same ingredients used in the Amazon, but I have found an alternative available in most of the western world. The main purpose of the flower bath is to bring healing energy to our mental, emotional and psychic space. As we clear the emotions associated with wounds or trauma, we need to fill these spaces with high-frequency energy. Because the aromatic flowers used in this practice vibrate with that energy, this soothing bath fills us with the healing energy to mend our wounds.

Traditionally, rose petals (they can be dry) and fresh marigolds (leaves and flowers) are soaked in a 3- to 5-gallon bucket of water. If you have only one type of flower, that's fine, but combining both will be more powerful. In the morning, immerse the flowers and leaves in the water and break them apart. Leave them to soak until evening. As with the body scrub, use the plant material to scrub your body, and finish by pouring the flower water over your head and body. Allow yourself to air dry so the essences of the flowers penetrate your skin.

· · ·

This works great in the Amazon, where the weather is warm. In colder climates, I recommend soaking the flowers in a hot bath for ten minutes prior to your immersion. Technically, we are making a tea to soak in. I like this method, because you can sit longer in the water, and the flower essences penetrate deeper into your being. Make sure to break the flowers into small pieces with your hands, and use a filter bag for the plant material to avoid clogging your plumbing. Take a flower bath anytime you need a boost in energy. It relaxes the body, brings healing to the emotional space, soothes the soul, and increases vitality.

CONNECTING THE DOTS

I HAVE PRESENTED these concepts in a strategic way. We started with the inner foundation, because it is the fundamental first step. It's pointless to address our wounds, traumas, and conditioning if we lack the inner structure that will help support our healing. It takes time, work, and effort to go through an emotional release process. If we engage in the process of healing our traumas without having properly cultivated the Universal Principles, we will add unnecessary work to our process. Commitment, integrity, respect, honesty, compassion, courage, patience, and forgiveness constitute the foundation of true healing. Healing is supported by our regular daily practices, which we rely on in challenging times.

We must go through the emotional release process multiple times before fully addressing the backlog of unresolved situations from the past. Remember, following your spiritual path is a lifelong journey. We cannot expect to address 20-30 years of life experiences in a few months. It might take several years, because we can't speed up the process. If we move too quickly, we will fall back into old behaviors, ensuring more work for ourselves. We must also be able to function in daily life and give ourselves the time, as well as the physical and emotional space, we need to work, be present with our families, and attend to other responsibilities. Each time you go through an emotional release process, don't be too quick to move on to the next thing; wait until you feel strong, and you are able to live the lessons you gathered.

Bamboo grows by sealing segments as it sprouts upward. In the same way, we want to seal healing and wisdom into ourselves before we start another emotional release process. Again, follow your intuition. There is no need to rush the process, for the lessons we need are right here before us. Focusing on the present, we will discover lessons that keep the healing process moving forward naturally. When in doubt, wait until you feel a strong "yes" from your intuition; that is the time to begin the next stage of your healing journey.

Please don't forget to keep a light-hearted attitude towards yourself and your process. This is not the military, so don't take yourself too seriously. Find humor as you move through your emotional and spiritual development. Humor adds positive energy, helping you move through stagnation and fueling your momentum. You will need the clarity of mind that humor brings in order to connect your life experiences with the spiritual and emotional patterns they have generated, which will open the door for deeper wisdom to arise.

. . .

So far, I have talked about the process of spiritual development without discussing elements of Indigenous practices. Not everyone feels called to include such practices in their inner work. There are many paths to follow when we climb our own mountain of wisdom, each with its benefits and challenges. Your intuition will guide you to the path that best resonates with you. In the following chapter, I present an introduction to the Indigenous practices I have experienced over the last 12 years. Please understand that you will need appropriate guidance if you wish to dive deeper into the world of Indigenous traditions and experience them yourself.

CHAPTER IV

ANCIENT INDIGENOUS WISDOM

"Everything on the earth has a purpose, every disease an herb to cure it, and every person a mission. This is the Indian theory of existence."

— Christal Quintasket - Salish

EARTH-BASED TRADITIONAL INDIGENOUS PRACTICES

We need to create a new reality for humanity. We modern humans have developed incredible technology, but we have disregarded its environmental toll. At the same time, we possess ancient technologies, developed by Indigenous people, that resonate fully with nature. We can't go back in time and let go of all our advances in technology. However, we need to weave modern and ancient technologies together to develop a new society, one which values nature, community, and spiritual development, rather than the greed of the capitalist system.

Throughout my travels, I have been exposed to different Indigenous traditions, practices which continue to support my spiritual development today. According to the Indigenous cosmology, only people who have faced their fears and demons (wounds, conditioning, and traumas) are able to see their paths with clarity and certainty. People in Indigenous communities engage in ceremonies using master medicine plants. These plants and trees have the capacity to transmit wisdom during rituals, ceremonies, and initiations, allowing participants to cleanse themselves of negative emotions, limited views, and to receive direction from their spirit guides and ancestors.

Some of these rituals are simple and easy to perform alone. Others, especially those using master medicine plants, require the guidance of an experienced shaman or medicine man/woman to safely navigate the journey and avoid potential risks. These rituals open the energetic door to other realms. They also open deep personal processes; this can make people inexperienced in such processes vulnerable to manipulation by ill-intentioned entities. The shaman or medicine man/woman has the tools to open an energetic door safely, creating a physical and psychic space undisturbed by external influences to ensure the protection of everyone within such space.

Conducted with experienced guidance, these rituals have the potential to be incredibly healing. However, when people use sacred Indigenous medicines without the necessary tools to navigate spiritual realms, they risk facing situations they are unable to handle. For instance, they may attract unwanted entities into their psychic spaces. These energies can negatively influence the person in subtle and stealthy ways. Experiencing such a deep process without the proper guidance can also negatively alter one's grasp on reality. Because there is great power associated with these rituals, they have a huge potential for healing; but they have an equally huge potential to harm. Therefore, it is imperative to properly prepare for these rituals and to participate in them only with trusted, trained facilitators.

AROMATIC ESSENCES
TRADITIONALLY USED FOR
CLEARING: THE PRACTICE OF
SMUDGING

INDIGENOUS PEOPLES from North and South America use wildcrafted essences, which are considered sacred, to clear negative energies from the body, mind, and spirit, as well as from places. Native Americans commonly burn white sage (Salvia apiana) or white prairie sage (Artemisia ludoviciana) for energy clearing purposes. Traditionally, the sage is burned in an abalone shell, and a feather is used to fan the smoke onto the person or place in need of clearing. This practice is called smudging. When gatherings require clarity of mind, body and spirit, each participant is smudged before entering the already cleared gathering space. The smoke of the burnt sage clears negative energy from spaces: a room, an office, or a home. It also clears negative energy from our mental, emotional, and psychic spaces. Wherever we use sage, whether to clear a place or ourselves, an energy emptiness is created. Therefore, it is important and traditional to burn sweetgrass (Hierochloe odorata) after smudging with sage to replace the emptiness with positive energy. We can use the smudging practice to support our inner work when we do an emotional release process or a fire ritual, or when we need to clear our mental, emotional or psychic space after a stressful day.

Cedar leaves are another staple essence used by Native Americans. Many different species of cedar trees are used for smudging. It is believed the smoked of burned cedar invites positive energy and protects a space (physical, mental, emotional, or psychic). The cedar tree is highly revered by Native Americans, who use it for many other purposes, in addition to smudging.

Tobacco (nicotiana tabacum and nicotiana rustica) is one of the plants most misunderstood by modern society. The tobacco I refer to is unrefined and unprocessed, completely different from the tobacco in commercial cigarettes. Across the Americas, tobacco is highly revered by Indigenous people, who consider it a sacred and powerful plant teacher. Native Americans use tobacco during prayer, as the smoke is believed to carry prayers to the Creator. When smoked in prayer, tobacco smoke is not inhaled into the lungs. Rather, it is kept in the mouth and exhaled. A small amount of tobacco is left as an offering when harvesting plants or collecting feathers or shells, to honor the spirit of the plant or animal and as an energy exchange. Indigenous peoples in South America have similar practices, leaving small amounts of tobacco at the base of a plant when harvesting it. Since the variety of tobacco used in South America is stronger than the North American variety, Indigenous people there use it for energy clearing purposes by blowing its smoke onto people or places that need energy clearing. It is also ingested in different forms, such as a tea for connecting with the tobacco spirit, or a powder, which is blown onto the nose to induce a trance, enabling the user to gather wisdom from the spirit world during a ceremony.

In South America the dried resin of the copal tree (protium copal) is used the way sage is in North America. Pieces of the dried resin are put onto coals, creating a rich, aromatic smoke which is fanned around a person or place in need of cleansing from negative or unwanted energies. It is also used in clearing rituals and healing ceremonies. To fill the resulting energy void, dried pieces of the Palo Santo tree (Bursera graveolens) are burned afterwards. (However, if you have access to it, it's better to use cedar, instead, as Palo Santo's increasing popularity has created a high level of demand for the tree, and it's being cut down at an alarming rate.)

FIRE RITUALS

MANY TRADITIONS HAVE a special relationship with the fire. It is used in different rituals as a powerful ally, teacher, and guide. Each tradition has unique protocols that honor and respect the fire within the context of the ritual or ceremony in which it is used. The common theme among these traditions is the importance of working with intention around the fire. When approaching the fire, we must also ask for help with respect and humility. We need to be aware around the fire, or we might burn ourselves or others. Native Americans regard the fire as the grandfather, because it is old, wise, and demands respect. We must maintain this awareness as we work with the fire, moving coals and logs with intention and respect. For the Mayans, the fire ceremony opens a portal to the spirit world, from which healing, guidance, blessings, transformation, and growth can flow.

· · ·

Fire has an incredible transformative quality. Any substance put into the fire experiences a profound transformation. When used with intention, and approached with reverence and respect, the fire is an incredible ally that can help us burn and transform emotions. I use the aid of the fire when I have a great deal of emotions floating around in my mental, emotional, and psychic space. As I sit and meditate with the fire, I ask for its help to transform the thoughts and emotions associated with the issue I am confronting. After a few hours in the presence of the fire, I always feel lighter and more centered. Powerful lessons are also revealed in the process.

The following ritual does not belong to a particular tradition but has all the elements to create a proper physical space for doing inner work and developing a respectful relationship with the fire and its transformative energy.

A proper physical space for a fire ritual is outdoors, in a place where you are not going to be disturbed, and you are not going to disturb anyone else. An appropriate fireplace indoors could also work. Check and follow local regulations and fire restrictions. Also, be aware of weather and wind conditions. Strong winds can be dangerous if you have a fire. Always consider safety first. Don't light a fire in a place where you could start a forest fire, or too close to a house. A raised fireplace with a metal screen cover is a perfect set-up for safely lighting your fire. Additionally, I recommend making sure you have a hose or other source of water nearby, in case you need to prevent the fire from getting out of control.

. . .

The first step in the ritual is to have a clear intention. Check the lunar calendar and use the new moon or full moon to set a date for your ritual. Offer cedar leaves to the fire as a gesture of gratitude for the help that will be provided. You can do the ritual alone, or with like-minded friends who want to do inner work. Avoid conversations during the ritual; silence will help you to be fully present and open to the lessons that will arise. Lay out your firewood in a neat and orderly fashion. You don't need a huge fire; logs of two inches in diameter are sufficient. Gather also a good amount of dry thin branches and twigs. Dried leaves can be used as kindling, in addition to the twigs.

Once your firewood is ready to light, every participant expresses their intentions aloud. Afterwards, light the fire. Once the fire is stable, do an offering of cedar leaves. They will burn and flare up quickly but also settle quickly. Now, focus on the situation associated with the wound or trauma to allow its emotions to surface. Ask silently for the fire's help in transforming and transmuting the negative emotions. Pay close attention to what the fire is doing, and to what you are feeling and thinking. A sudden break of a log, or unprovoked shift in the flames, represents a sign from the fire. What were you thinking or feeling at that moment? How does that connect to the wound or trauma? Allow yourself to be guided by the fire. You can use cedar leaves again at this point in the ritual, offering them to the fire after you express your prayers and blessings. Praying in this manner is powerful, so be mindful and specific about what you ask.

As you move through the ritual, you will reach a point when you are ready to release your emotions into the fire. Before you do so, let the fire know your intention, and offer gratitude for the help provided. Again, use cedar after your release is finished to give thanks to the fire and to offer blessings and healing for everybody involved. If you journaled about your emotions prior to the ritual, and feel the need to let go of your writing, you can burn the pages that you wrote. After you have released your emotions, stop feeding the fire. You can continue to do offerings or prayers with cedar by putting it on the coals. At some point towards the end, put a good handful of cedar on the coals, and put yourself in the path of the smoke to smudge yourself. Make sure to expose your front and back to the smoke. When you feel complete, cover the flames with the metal screen, and allow the fire to die down by itself.

This ritual is powerful and simple. You can do it every new moon, every full moon, on solstices, equinoxes, or whenever you feel the need for it. It is a beautiful way of creating time to tune in with yourself and be away from the distractions of day-to-day life. As you develop your personal relationship with the fire, you will learn to read its signs and appreciate the ancient power hidden within the flames.

TRADITIONAL INDIGENOUS
CEREMONIES

INDIGENOUS PEOPLE around the world have developed unique rituals or ceremonies that help participants connect with their souls, heal emotional or spiritual wounds, receive guidance, communicate with the spirit world, and purify the mind, body and spirit. Each tribe has a particular way of conducting its rituals. There are a million ways to find truth, and no tradition is above the others. The variety and diversity of traditions account for the endless permutations of energy patterns that humans carry.

As I noted earlier, we originate from tribal societies where rituals were part of the culture. During the past twenty years, interest in traditional Indigenous rituals and ceremonies has grown exponentially, because of their healing potential. All these traditional practices alter the consciousness of the participants. Some involve the use of psychotropic plants, while others use no such substances. These rituals pre-date Western civilization and have been used worldwide to help cultivate inner development, healing, and connection with creation. Indigenous peoples regard these rituals or ceremonies as medicine.

Traditional rituals cannot be studied objectively, as a scientist might. Rather, they must be experienced directly to be understood. Many times, the ritual initiates a process that takes months, or even years, to complete. Below are just a few examples of the rituals humans have used since pre-modern times in the quest to connect with their souls. I have participated in all the rituals described. Your intuition will guide you towards the path that best resonates with you.

THE SWEAT LODGE

THE SWEAT LODGE uses all four elements to create a powerful ritual for clearing heavy emotions, purifying the body of toxins, and opening a portal of communication with the spirit world. It is also known as the Inipi or Temazcal and is practiced widely throughout North America and Mexico.

The ritual is held in a lodge made of fresh branches, which is then covered with blankets. Just outside is a fire and an altar. Each tradition creates the altar in a unique way, with specific prayers, and a particular protocol specifying how people enter the lodge. Hours before the ritual starts, volcanic rocks are stacked neatly, and a fire is built around them. When the rocks are hot enough, people gather and enter the lodge following specific protocols.

. . .

The lodge is small and dark. It feels like you are in the womb of your mother again. You enter by crawling on your hands and knees. A deep connection to the earth comes from the ritual. Once every participant is inside, the fire man brings in a particular number of hot rocks. Then the door is closed. The medicine man or woman in charge of the ritual begins pouring small amounts of water onto the rocks, which creates steam. Certain essences are placed on the rocks to clean, support, and bring positive energies into the ceremonial space.

Each medicine person uses a set of healing songs to protect the space, open a connection with the spirit world, and bring healing energy into the lodge. The songs represent the air, completing the elemental circle of fire, water, earth, and air. The songs, combined with the strong heat, allows participants to enter an altered state of consciousness where profound healing can happen. After a number of songs and pours of water, the door is opened. Normally, people won't leave the lodge, but some may need to cool off outside before the next round of the ritual starts. Depending on the tradition, the ritual lasts for three or four rounds of the process described above. After the last round, everyone comes out according to protocol, and the ritual ends. People cool off and rest. Then the lodge is cleaned and, typically, a meal is shared.

The sweat lodge is a powerful ritual. The heat can get intense, but it can bring deep healing and clarity. It is particularly effective in cleaning old emotions and stagnation. It is also used to send prayers to ancestors or the Creator. In order to facilitate this ritual properly, it is important that the leader has gone through the proper training and has been blessed to carry on such work. Most sweat lodges are by invitation only. When a participant is in need of healing, he or she requests a sweat lodge ritual by presenting tobacco as an offering to the medicine person who will conduct it. There is great intention in the prayers used throughout the ritual.

The first time I attended a sweat lodge, I was a bit nervous and excited at the same time. The nervousness wore off as I helped bring firewood to the site and dressed - put blankets on – the lodge. It took about two hours for the fire to properly heat up the rocks. Once the medicine person had completed preparations for the ritual, participants were invited inside the lodge. After we all crawled in, the heated volcanic rocks were brought in, one by one, until the desired number of rocks was reached. As the rocks were brought in, I could feel the heat on my skin (I was just wearing shorts). After the door closed, the red rocks glowed eerily in the pitch-black lodge. I started to feel uncomfortable as the heat increased and water was poured over the rocks. Steam completely filled the lodge. As feelings of anger, frustration, emotional pain, and self-righteousness arose in my consciousness, I found myself going into a fetal position, with my head resting on the ground, which was the "coolest" place I could find. Then, when the songs started, my emotions began to shift. Slowly, I felt the songs helped to free myself from their grasp. The smell of the sweet grass burning on the rocks gave me comfort.

I was starting to feel overwhelmed by the heat and my emotions, when the door was opened. The first round had ended. The fresh air helped me tremendously. Five minutes later, the door was closed, and the second round began. Again, I found myself taking a fetal position to withstand the heat. I was still holding on to many of my emotions, but the intensity of the heat kept wearing me down. At the same time, the songs continued to offer support. I felt held by their melody, and the scent of the essences also comforted me. After what felt an eternity – it was around fifteen minutes – the door was opened again, ending the second round. This time I felt more tired and relieved than I had after the first round.

Shortly afterwards, the third round began. When the songs restarted, I was too tired to keep holding on to my emotions, and I was finally able to release them. I felt an inner shift from all the emotional turmoil. Humbled by the power of what I was experiencing, I forgave myself and others involved in the situations that had been brought to my awareness during the ritual. It occurred to me that humans have been doing this ritual to purify themselves for generations. My feeling of humility kept growing. There was so much to learn, I felt, and so much I was not aware of. After the fourth round was finished, I was incredibly tired, and I stepped out of the lodge into fresh air again. There was a hose nearby, where people were refreshing themselves. I put the hose on my head and allowed the water to cool my body. After eating some food, I slept soundly for two hours.

I came upon the sweat lodge tradition during a time when I was diving deep into my upbringing and carried unresolved wounds from my childhood and teenage years. The intensity of the heat, the songs, and the post-ritual peace all brought relief to my soul. The power of the heat wore down my anger, self-right-eousness, and stubborn attitude, opening the door to a deeper understanding of my past. This allowed me to start exploring my past in search of lessons and healing. Although the sweat lodge helped me tremendously, it is definitely not for everyone. The heat and the tight physical space can be challenging for people who aren't ready to look at their emotional wounds, or who suffer from claustrophobia.

TRADITIONAL PLANT MEDICINE CEREMONIES

IN THIS SECTION, I introduce plant medicine and describe how it has been traditionally used by some Indigenous peoples. From an Indigenous perspective, these plants are sacred medicines, and for the purposes of this book, I connect their use with inner development work and explain the benefits I have experienced. More extensive information about these Indigenous groups and their ritual use of plants is available in books and research studies. I encourage you to read further about the topics that interest you.

The use of Peyote by Native Americans in the southwestern region of the US and in northern Mexico predates colonial times. This cactus is a powerful psychedelic master medicine plant with the ability to heal the mind, body, and spirit. It is also used as a powerful way of praying to ancestors and the Creator, establishing a line of communication from the higher spheres of the spiritual planes to the participants of the ritual. Among tribes that use Peyote, it is always viewed as medicine given by the earth to heal humans. From a tribal point of view, most modern people have been sickened by their disconnect from the cycles of nature. A sacred medicine, Peyote can restore that connection and heal the transgressions of our modern way of life. The healing potential is huge when we understand the intentions behind its ingestion and the ceremony used to consume it. Peyote survived colonial times because tribes hid it from conquerors.

The use of Ayahuasca among Indigenous people of South America also predates colonial times and is still widely used by numerous tribes today. Ayahuasca is a strong psychedelic master medicine plant; it brings healing of the mind, body, and spirit. It has traditionally been used to open a portal of communication with the guardian spirits of the jungle in order to ask their permission to hunt game and grow food. It also has been used to connect with celestial beings for healing and to receive universal wisdom. The visionary states reached during an Ayahuasca journey allow the shaman to diagnose a disease and determine which plants would aid in healing a patient's ailment. As with Peyote in North America, the use of Ayahuasca went underground during colonial times, and only began to be used openly again towards the end of the last century.

The bad reputation typically associated with sacred plant medicines originates in ideas spread by the Catholic church during colonial times. The church referred to sacred plants used in rituals across the Americas as the work of the devil.

Such ideas have been passed down, generation after generation, until very recently, despite reputable studies demonstrating the powerful healing capacities of these plants.

Participating in master medicine plant ceremonies allows an opportunity to connect to the deepest parts of ourselves, heal from traumatic events, and experience a tangible connection with the cosmos and creation. For master medicine plants to provide their full benefit, they must be used in a traditional, ceremonial context. These medicines have not been processed in a lab; rather, they have been harvested from a natural setting, ensuring the purity of the energies released during their use. Research has shown that most people using sacred medicines in the context of a traditional ceremony experience major breakthroughs in their healing process. When using these plants, it is paramount to stay within the context of such a tradition, so as to avoid adverse results.

Ceremonies using sacred medicines are not for everybody. We must each determine the appropriate practice to heal our wounds, conditioning, or trauma, understanding that whichever process we choose will allow us to find the lessons we need to learn. However, I am describing these particular traditions because they have the potential to help many people. Again, it is important to cultivate our intuition, which allows us to contemplate information presented to us and determine whether or not it aligns with ourselves.

THE PEYOTE CEREMONY

As NOTED EARLIER, each tradition has a unique way of conducting ceremonies. The Peyote ceremonies I attended were held by Cheyenne and Lakota people. These ceremonies are typically requested by someone who needs healing, or who has specific prayer requests, and are initiated by that person, who offers tobacco to the medicine man and asks him to lead the ceremony. Community support and collective prayer are vital components of the Peyote ceremony. Traditionally, men oversee harvesting a particular type of firewood, cutting the logs to a specific length, and ridding it of small branches. The bark is also peeled off to avoid producing smoke inside the tipi, where the fire will burn throughout the ceremony. Men build the tipi as well, selecting a location for the structure that considers the four directions (east, west, north, south) in order to align the door with a particular cardinal point. Specific prayers are then placed on the tipi pole, behind the area where the medicine man sits. Women are in charge of preparing a feast to be shared after the ceremony. They are also responsible for saying certain prayers during the ceremony, which starts towards the end of the day and can last until mid-morning the following day (from 12-16 hours). A specific protocol is used to enter the tipi, and many others are used inside the tipi during the ceremony.

Once every participant is inside, the meeting starts. The fire has been started before participants enter the tipi. The space around the fire is designated as an altar, and a Peyote button is placed there. Someone is in charge of the fire all night long, tasked with the duty of keeping it burning at a constant rate while he spreads the coals into specific patterns. Once a pattern has been created, essences are sprinkled over the coals to clear and bless all participants. The sponsor who called the ceremony shares his or her situation aloud. After some prayers, and after certain protocols are followed, the Peyote is shared with all participants. It comes as fresh buttons, dried powder, or tea. Shortly afterwards, the songs start. The medicine man opens the ceremony with his songs before allowing anyone else to sing. Afterwards, each experienced participant has an opportunity to sing four songs, one for each direction. A rattle and a drum are used to accompany the songs. The singer uses the rattle, and there is a designated drummer for the entire night. The drummer moves around the tipi to sit next to the singer. The ceremony moves through periods of songs, prayer, and Peyote ingestion. Towards the middle of the ceremony, there is special prayer for the water. In the morning, before the closing of the ceremony, there is a special prayer for the food.

The second time I participated in a Peyote ceremony, I connected deeply for the first time with the Peyote and the fire.

The ceremony was for a friend of mine, and I felt a sense of purpose as I helped set up the tipi and harvested and cleaned firewood. The sense of community during this preparation was beautiful to experience. The preparations take place in the days leading to the ceremony; with them, excitement and anticipation was building in me. My friend is well known in the area, and many people showed up. In fact, there were so many people that a second location was quickly prepared to hold those who would not fit in the first tipi. Needless to say, we were packed close together inside (about 40 of us were inside). The fire had been burning since the afternoon, and we were invited in as the sunset light was dimming. I had been instructed in some of the protocols but had to remained alert, to make sure I was following the lead of other, more experienced participants in the tipi.

When the Peyote was passed to me, I ingested a fresh piece, which was quite bitter. Then, mustering my courage, I served myself an entire spoonful of dried Peyote powder. The powder was not easy to swallow and was also quite bitter, sending cold waves down my spine. Last, I drank Peyote tea, to help me swallow any remainders of the powder. Compared to the other forms, the tea was mildly bitter. Once everyone had partaken of the Peyote, the songs began. Slowly, I started to feel a shift in my awareness. Mostly I focused on the fire, but every so often, my eyes wandered around to inspect what was happening elsewhere in the tipi. The warmth of the fire was comforting as the night cooled, and the effects of the Peyote started to intensify. My senses felt more attuned to the people around me, the songs, and the fire. The intensity kept escalating, taking me to a place where words were unnecessary. I was still fully present physically, but my psychic self was fully opened. With the increased effects of the Peyote, my eyes were fixated on the fire. I could feel the power behind the songs, and how they resonated with the fire. A sense of ancestral connection arose from the fire. It was similar to what I felt when I visited my grandfather, who had passed away nine years earlier. Now, I felt that an aspect of him was coming through the fire to teach and guide me. Tears fell from my eyes; I hadn't realized that the lack of a grandfatherly presence in my life had resulted in such emptiness within me. Although my other grandfather was still alive, I'd felt more of a connection with the one that died.

While I was experiencing these profound realizations, the ceremony was getting more intense. People were being scolded for misbehavior; I could feel the fire man's anger at these transgressions, and now most people were unsettled. I started to feel increasingly frustrated and insulted by the distractions. Shortly after these disturbances, dried cedar leaves were offered to the fire to cleanse the agitated feelings and emotions. A woman directed by the roadman – the ceremony leader – offered a prayer, and soon the energy of the space settled into the rhythms of the songs. All the while, my grandfather kept guiding me to stay focused on the fire, release the emotions, and ask for the help and support of the fire to transform them. The ceremony progressed, with more Peyote passed around for consumption, more songs and prayers. It reached a point where I felt no need to ingest more Peyote. The sense of connection with my grandfather and the fire increased as the night progressed. I also felt strongly connected with myself, my inner power, and my commitment to respect the ceremony in which I was participating. It was not until mid-morning of the following day that we emerged from the tipi. As I stepped outside into the sunlight, I felt permeated by a feeling of accomplishment.

. . .

Peyote is an incredible medicine, capable of opening a powerful, and real, connection with the fire. During the ceremony there is a strong synergy between the Peyote, the fire and the songs. Peyote is known as the grandfather medicine for its strong masculine energy, and through the long nights in the tipi during the ceremonies, this medicine has taught me about finding my inner power. It's helped me build character by staying put, no matter what was happening inside of me, or in the ceremony. Observing the intentionality of every step and element of the ceremony has taught me respect for this medicine and the tradition built around its use. The most powerful teaching I experienced was seeing a community coming together to pray and help one individual, and the beauty that comes from such special moments.

THE AYAHUASCA CEREMONY

An Ayahuasca ceremony is completely different from a Peyote ceremony. Ayahuasca is regarded as the grandmother medicine for its feminine energy. Due to the nature of the Ayahuasca brew, proper dietary guidelines must be followed by all participants in the weeks leading up to the ceremony. The shaman is in charge of going into the jungle to find the ingredients to prepare the brew, a long, involved process. The final product is highly concentrated, so participants don't need to drink much to experience its effects. The ceremony is traditionally held in a maloca, or medicine house. Participants gather at sunset, and once the shaman deems everyone ready, the ceremony starts. Normally, the shaman has already met with each person to learn their intentions and personal situation. After prayers are said over the brew, everyone is served. Sacred silence is honored throughout the ceremony, which is held in the dark while the shaman sings Icaros, or healing songs, throughout the night. The songs create an energy protection and guide the journey. They are also sung to protect the participants and call-in certain plant and animal spirits. It is common for people to vomit during the ceremony. Ayahuasca is known for its cleansing qualities, and purging is seen as a way of ridding the body of toxic energies and emotions. There is a strong synergy between the songs and the effects of Ayahuasca in participants.

Although the ceremony is performed with a group of people, the experience itself is quite personal. It is normal for unresolved situations, traumas, and emotional or spiritual wounds to surface during the journey. Facing them enables us to bring healing energy to those wounded areas of our inner selves. Some of the effects of Ayahuasca can create a visionary experience, in which guidance about personal problems could be received. The ceremony can last from six to eight hours. The shaman determines when the closing of the ceremony takes place, once the effects have subsided in participants.

Twelve years after my first experiences with Ayahuasca, I still remember them vividly. I'd been feeling as though I was searching constantly for something – an experience beyond the ordinary – when my good friend Ricardo shared his experiences with Ayahuasca. Immediately, I felt a strong desire to participate in a ceremony.

After planning my trip for a couple of months, I found myself driving west of Caracas to the outskirts of another big city, Maracay. Tucked in a quiet neighborhood was a beautiful colonial-era house that had been selected as the site for the ceremony, which was being conducted by two taitas - ceremony leaders – from Colombia's Putumayo region. We set up our tents and socialized until 11p.m., when the ceremony started. One by one, each participant approached the altar where the Yagé – as Ayahuasca is known in Colombia and Ecuador - was being poured. The taita stared at each participant for a moment before deciding how much to pour. My turn finally arrived, and in a small gourd I received my portion, which I drank in one motion. The taste was bitter-sweet, giving me the sensation of chills running through my body. It took about five minutes for the taste to clear from my mouth. I settled into my chair and patiently waited for the effects to develop.

A little over an hour later, my perception of reality started shifting. Unlike my later experiences with Peruvian traditions, where songs are used throughout the night, this ceremony was conducted in silence. It took until the second serving for the effects of the Yagé to intensify. With my eyes closed, I started seeing visions generated by the Yagé. Also, an increasing discomfort in my stomach pushed me to feel some of my long-buried emotions. At first, I asked myself what I was doing in the ceremony. Then my emotions shifted, and I began to feel repressed anger. As the discomfort built, so did the anger. Eventually, I was able to vomit. Relief filled my being, and my anger gave way to thankfulness. I settled in my chair quite comfortably, grateful for the clearing that had happened.

Eventually, the third serving was offered. I felt a strong pull to get up and drink more. The Yagé settle in my stomach nicely, without any discomfort. An hour later, I found myself in the same emotional place as before, with increased nausea and discomfort. These conditions allowed the anger to arise again, until it culminated in another round of vomiting. By the time I gathered myself together, the sun was rising, and musicians were getting ready to play. The music was beautiful, beyond what I can describe. For the next two hours, Andean rhythms filled the early morning air, inspiring feelings of hope, renewal, and healing.

Around 8 a.m., the ceremony concluded. Most participants had a light breakfast, and socializing began again. Five hours later, we gathered for the next ceremony. I received a smaller portion this time than I had the previous night, but it proved to be all I needed. During the daytime, nature becomes incredibly attractive under the effects of the Yagé. As its effects intensified, I felt an increasing connection to all of creation. When I closed my eyes, vivid visions reflected the feelings I was experiencing. It was one of the most unforgettable experiences of my life. More servings were offered, but I felt no need to move from my seat. The initial four hours were conducted in silence, until the musicians broke it with beautiful melodies, while I basked in an incredible, expansive feeling of connection.

In my experiences with Ayahuasca, I have been blessed with healing, major lessons, and beautiful guidance for my life. I learned about the power of my words when used constructively, or destructively. I experienced being on the receiving end of my anger, which helped me release trapped emotions within myself. I learned how to put myself in someone else's shoes to understand their situation; this has allowed me to understand the energy dynamics of people and situations more deeply. I learned that unless I cultivate self-love, I can't love anybody else. I learned that life is never a straight path, but rather a winding road that takes us to extraordinary places. And I learned about patience. This was difficult, because in order for me to learn about patience, I needed to be patient! I learned that everything that I experience is my responsibility, and if I need to change something, I have to work on it. I learned to see challenges as opportunities to learn, grow, and do inner work. I learned about cultivating the Universal Principles to build a solid inner foundation for myself. Many of the lessons shared in this book come from my months of isolation in the middle of the Amazon, participating in Ayahuasca ceremonies.

FINAL THOUGHTS

THE IDEAS, concepts, and perspectives I have shared with you have taken me 12 years to experience. As I began to assemble individual pieces, it felt as if I was putting together a puzzle, without having a picture of the final product. But as I continued, I found points of connection between these pieces, and slowly, the picture started to emerge. I wrote this book with the intention of helping people connect more deeply with themselves. A deeper inner connection brings to the surface the wounds, conditioning, and traumas we must face to bring healing, transformation, and growth into our lives. As we do our inner work, we develop foresight and intuition, which allows us to see our unique path on this planet with more clarity.

Each person has a life purpose that emerges as we heal and grow. The more of us that awaken to our inner calling, the stronger and faster true change can be achieved on a global level. If there was ever a time when humans needed to focus on their own personal history, it is now. If each person on this planet focused on healing their wounds, conditioning, and traumas, a major shift in the consciousness of the world would occur. The climate crisis, the pandemic, and the global demonstrations for racial equality are all signs that we need to change quickly in order to preserve this precious planet. Such beauty comes from humans healing their traumas. Imagine a world where human lives and natural resources are valuable assets, not disposable numbers. All it takes is a shift in perspective.

Indigenous people carry with them incredible sacred medicines and ceremonial traditions. They are changing people's perspectives and healing their wounds. If you feel called to commune with these medicines, and receive lessons during this experience, it is imperative to integrate them into your life, otherwise, true healing won't occur. We can all learn from the Indigenous peoples of this earth, who carry unwritten books of knowledge about their environments and how to thrive in balance with nature. In contrast, our progress, development, and way of life represent the destruction of the environment. We must change that equation. Only when our leaders have healed their own wounds, conditioning, or traumas, will humanity be able to change the course of our current destructive path and begin a new journey towards regeneration, conservation, balance, and peace.

APPENDIX

Breathing Exercises

There are countless types of breathing exercises, so try a variety of techniques to find the one that resonate most with you. The following exercise is called Nadhi Sodhana. It comes from the ancient yogic traditions of pranayama, which means "extending life force" in Sanskrit. The alternating nature of the exercise brings balance to our being, calms the nervous system, and oxygenates our bodies, enabling our cells to function properly. It is a great tool to reduce stress and bring harmony to mind, body, and spirit.

- Sitting upright on a chair, or on the floor, take three deep breaths.

- With your right thumb, press down on your right nostril and inhale only through your left nostril. The inhalation should be slow and steady. Use your diaphragm to fill your lungs to capacity.

- Release your thumb and use your index finger to press on your left nostril, so you exhale only through your right nostril. Make sure to exhale completely.

- Keep your index finger pressing your left nostril and inhale fully only through the right nostril.

- Release the index finger and press the right nostril with your thumb to exhale fully only through your left nostril. This constitutes one cycle. You inhale and exhale once through both nostrils.

- Start with 3-5 cycles and work your way to 10 cycles.

- After you have finished the exercise, release it and allow normal breathing to return. Bask in the calm and peace this exercise can bring. This exercise is a great prelude for meditation.

———

Meditation

Just as with breathing exercises, there are countless techniques for meditation. Once again, I encourage you to experiment with different techniques, in order to find the ones that resonate deeply with you.

. . .

One meditation technique that works for me is the repetition of a mantra. A mantra is a phrase or sound that helps meditation. It is repeated for a period of time and then released, allowing one to drop into a deep meditative space. This technique has ancient roots in Buddhism and Hinduism. A quick search on the internet will bring up a long list of mantras, along with their meanings. Use the one that most resonates with you. The mantras have specific vibrations that help calm and focus the mind, so all static thoughts fade out of your consciousness.

You can repeat the mantra inwardly, or out loud. I like repeating the mantra out loud, because something powerful comes from feeling in my body the vibration of the mantra I am uttering. This is the Buddhist mantra I use. It's called the heart sutra:

"GATE GATE PARAGATE PARASAMGATE BODHI SVAHA OM"

Translated from Sanskrit, it means: "Oh awakening that has gone, gone, gone to the further shore, gone completely to the further shore."

After doing your breathing exercises, you have set the psychic space to start a meditation. I recommend using a timer with a gentle ringer for 10 minutes as you repeat your mantra. After you release the mantra, give yourself 5-10 minutes to bask in the peaceful vibration cultivated through your practice. Keep in mind that you can also use affirmations as a mantra. Or, after you have come out of your meditation, you can repeat the affirmations out loud at least three times.

Affirmations

Below are examples of affirmations relating to each chakra. I encourage you to personalize them, according to what you are working on. Play around with different affirmations to get a feel for the one that resonates most strongly with you. Repeat the affirmations daily until you have overcome the block or healed the wound. At first, it might be uncomfortable to repeat some affirmations. Be patient; as you slowly create a new program in your consciousness, you will open the channel to return to balance.

Consistency is important when using affirmations. The best way to work with them is to use them every day as part of your meditation practice. You can go through the breathing exercises and mantra meditation, then finish with affirmations. I like to repeat each affirmation that I am working with at least three times. You don't need to repeat the affirmations for the rest of your life, just for a period of time. Eventually, through repetition, you will begin to embody the affirmation, a process that occurs at different points for each person. Keep working with the affirmation until you feel strong in the area on which you are focusing your attention. Here are samples of affirmations that address each of the chakras.

First chakra

- I connect deeply with the healing energy of the earth.
- I am supported by the universe and provided with all I need to heal, grow, and thrive.
- I connect deeply with the grounding energy of the earth.
- I am grounded, rooted, and centered.
- I honor my body and care for its needs deeply.

Second Chakra

- I surround myself with people that respect me, honor me and appreciate me for who I am.
- I give myself permission to express my creativity freely.
- I allow myself to enjoy my sexual energy and sex in a healthy way.
- I give myself permission to enjoy pleasure in my life.
- I honor, respect, and connect with my creative energy.

Third Chakra

- I give myself permission to step into my power confidently.
- I trust deeply in my inner power.
- I have the power to change my current situation.
- I use my power with honesty, respect and integrity.
- I have the power to commit to my inner development with discipline, consistency, and perseverance.

Fourth Chakra

- I love myself. I forgive myself. Thank you for my life today.
- I give myself permission to open my heart to eternal love.
- I walk through life with an open heart.
- I allow my heart to guide my life.
- I trust deeply in the guidance that comes from my heart.

Fifth Chakra

- I speak my truth clearly and eloquently, from a space of purity.
- I develop a balance between speaking my truth and listening to others' truth.
- I give myself permission to express my feelings and emotions in a constructive way.
- I allow myself to express my creativity with beauty and love.
- I am in tune with the energy I create with my words.

Sixth Chakra

- I give myself permission to trust deeply in my intuition.
- I see the challenges of my life as opportunities to learn and grow.
- I allow myself to develop my psychic abilities.
- I connect and follow my purpose in life.
- I can see with clarity, and without a doubt, my path on this earth.

Seventh Chakra

- I allow myself to be in constant connection with the Creator.
- I am guided by my higher self.
- I commune with the eternal and divine love that permeates throughout creation.
- I connect deeply with the divine within me.
- I am love. I am peace. I am divine. I am balanced.

Contemplation Practice

An excellent practice for inner development is spending time in nature. When I need to clear my thoughts, or be surrounded by a peaceful and balanced environment, I might go on a hike through the woods or mountains, spend time by a river, or connect with the wind or ocean. The main purpose of such outings is to contemplate nature. I like to do this on my own, in order to avoid being distracted by conversation. When we focus our attention on nature, we begin to embody its balanced state. Remember that nature is always resonating in perfect harmony with creation. Before you set out on your contemplation, state your intention of connecting with the trees, the wind, the river, the mountain, the valley, or the ocean. To establish an energy connection with nature by being present and attentive, focus on whatever aspect of nature grabs your attention, even if it's just a small leaf. Try to allow yourself to experience the peacefulness and beauty of the natural setting without expectations. Even if no great revelations occur, and you emerge from the experience simply feeling more peaceful, the time in contemplation allows you to slow your normal pace and return to balance. You can

FROM WOUND TO WISDOM

also use time in nature to let go of emotions. Trees have powerful grounding energy. Sitting by a tree, you can ask for help to transform certain energies, or ask permission to release what no longer serves you. The tree understands the energy behind your speech. As you express your intention and ask for permission, an energy connection is established with the tree. You can do this with a river, the ocean, the wind, the desert, etc. You will connect most easily in a place that resonates with you. You can also do the emotional release process in a natural setting, if you feel the environment is suited to you. It is important that no one disturbs you. Make sure that the natural area where you go is safe. Take appropriate precautions if there are wild animals around, and make sure that you can find your way back home.

Visualizations

There are many kinds of visualizations. Do some research and try different styles to find the one that resonates with you. All visualizations have a purpose, so make sure the visualization you choose aligns with your intentions. The following visualization exercises can help in your inner development process.

Grounding Visualization

This visualization is powerful when you are feeling ungrounded, you find yourself easily distracted, or when you are experiencing strong emotions. There are various versions on the internet, so feel free to try other grounding visualizations if this one does not resonate strongly with you.

· · ·

I like to do this visualization sitting on a chair. Make sure you are barefoot and that your back is straight.

- Close your eyes and take five deep breaths.

- Allow your breath to come naturally for a few moments before starting the visualization.

- Visualize a beam of light the width of your hips coming out of the base of your spine.

- See this beam of light penetrating the earth beneath you and going through the many layers until it reaches the core of the earth.

- Feel the grounding power of this connection. Through this channel, you can release energies and emotions that no longer serve you.

- As you hold that vision of your grounding channel, visualize the energy of the earth coming up through the soles of your feet, traveling through your legs and spine, reaching your head, and coming down the front of your body and out through your grounding channel. The energy flows from the earth, through your body and out the grounding channel.

- Now, visualize a beam of light coming from the sun and entering through the top of your head, traveling through your spine, and out your grounding channel.

- Hold that vision for 15 minutes. You can use affirmations like: "I am grounded, centered and balanced." Or you can personalize an affirmation for the specific process you are going through.

- The grounding channel will provide an outlet for releasing energies and emotions when you are doing the emotional release process.

- When you feel complete, take five deep breaths and open your eyes. Drink some water to bring yourself back completely into your body.

- If you have a hard time holding the entire exercise in your vision, start with just the grounding channel. When you can attain that visualization easily, add the part in which you bring earth energy up through your feet. Once you can visualize these two parts together, you can add the vision of connecting with the sun's energy.

Separation Visualization

This visualization exercise is used to create an energy separation between yourself and another person, place, or object. It can be used to cut energy cords, as well. The grounding visualization can be done prior to the separation visualization. This visualization is helpful when you want to reframe an existing relationship, or you are separating from someone you don't want in your life. I used this visualization to cut unhealthy cords with my mom and establish new ways of relating with her.

-Start by sitting upright on a chair barefoot.

- Close your eyes and take five deep breaths.

- Allow your breath to come naturally for a few moments before starting the visualization.

- Visualize yourself with the person you wish to separate from, or cut cords with. Imagine they are sitting in front of you. State your desire for separation, with the intention to bring healing to you and the person from whom you are separating.

- Now, visualize a marigold between the two of you. As you hold this vision, state that you let go of the person's energy, releasing it into the marigold. Use the full name of the person.

- While visualizing the same marigold still floating between you, summon your energy from the other person's psychic space. Visualize your energy returning to the marigold and being safely stored there.

- Visualize a fire between the two of you. Offer the marigold to the fire and say, "The eternal fire transforms our energies. My energy returns to me as healing energy. Your energy returns to you as healing energy." This constitutes one round. Repeat this visualization a total of seven times.

- If in your visualization you see an energy cord between yourself and the other person, visualize a gold sword, and imagine yourself striking the cord with the sword. Visualize the marigold drawing in all of the energy from the broken cord and offer it to the fire. State, "The eternal fire transforms our energies. My energy returns to me as healing energy. Your energy returns to you as healing energy."

- Visualize an eighth marigold. If the quality of the color is solid, the separation is complete. If you can see through the marigold, you will need to repeat the entire process at another time. Repeat this separation visualization once a day, until you are able to see the marigold as solid, without any translucent areas.

Offer the marigold to the fire and state, "I (your full name) am separated from (the other person's full name)" Repeat this out loud three times. When you feel complete, take five deep breaths and open your eyes. Drink some water to bring you back completely into your body. At this point, you can burn sage to clean your emotional and psychic space, followed by cedar to bring healing and blessings.

ACKNOWLEDGMENTS

I EXPRESS MY GRATITUDE, love, and admiration to my teacher and his family. They showed me a different world, one that I had been unaware of, and that brought me great healing, growth, and transformation. Through years of living and visiting them in the Amazon, their love, humor, and support has always been present.

Much love and gratitude to my mentor Monet Brooks. Her guidance, vision and support has always pointed me in right the direction. For 12 years she has always helped me through the many challenges of my path.

Much gratitude to my editors, including Kate Haas, for their support, inquisitive minds, and hard work. Through their insights, suggestions, and questions, they helped me improve the quality of the book tremendously.

Much gratitude to my parents, Maria and Salvatore, for all the positive values they instilled in me, which helped me navigate my life and harvest this book.

MUCHAS GRACIAS

Thank you for taking the time to read *From Wound to Wisdom*. If you enjoyed and found it meaningful, please consider leaving a review on the website of your favorite bookstore, or recommending my book to someone who can benefit from its message. As an independent author your review is greatly appreciated. To learn about future publications or events, please sign up for my email list at www.albertocurciolinares.com.

ABOUT THE AUTHOR

 Born and raised in Venezuela, Alberto Curcio Linares is a seeker with 20 years of experience in the area of spiritual development. After leaving his homeland as a young man, Alberto connected with the mystical world of Indigenous spiritual practices, living for years in the Peruvian Amazon and the Pacific Northwest while immersing himself in Indigenous traditions of healing and spirituality. The lessons acquired from these experiences inspired this book.

Now based in the jungle of Costa Rica, Alberto provides counseling sessions and spiritual support through the use of Indigenous practices. In his continued quest to live in harmony with the earth, uniting the physical with the spiritual, he is currently working on a homestead permaculture project.

Made in the USA
Monee, IL
22 September 2022

13664331R00125